MONTGOMERY LYALL

India: A Concise History Spanning Over 2000 Years

Copyright © 2025 by Montgomery Lyall

All rights reserved. No part of this publication may be reproduced, stored or transmitted in any form or by any means, electronic, mechanical, photocopying, recording, scanning, or otherwise without written permission from the publisher. It is illegal to copy this book, post it to a website, or distribute it by any other means without permission.

First edition

*This book was professionally typeset on Reedsy.
Find out more at reedsy.com*

Contents

1. India's Eternal Tapestry — 1
2. Dawn of Civilization – From the Indus to the Vedic Age — 10
3. Empires of Antiquity – Maurya and Gupta Dynasties — 20
4. Medieval Mosaic – Kingdoms, Invasions, and Syncretism — 29
5. The Mughal Legacy – Art, Architecture, and Administration — 40
6. Colonial Confluences – European Arrival and the British Raj — 50
7. The Freedom Struggle – Seeds of Nationalism and Revolution — 61
8. Partition and New Beginnings – The Birth of Modern Nations — 71
9. Building a Republic – India's Post-Colonial Transformation — 81
10. Unity in Diversity – Culture, Languages, and Regional... — 92
11. Contemporary India – Challenges, Triumphs, and Global... — 103
12. Reflections and the Road Ahead – India's Journey into the... — 114

1

India's Eternal Tapestry

India is often described as a land of timeless wonder—a subcontinent whose history spans thousands of years, imbued with diverse cultures, philosophies, and traditions. In this opening chapter, we embark on a journey to introduce the reader to India's multifaceted identity, setting the stage for a 2000-year narrative that is both informative and engaging. This chapter, "India's Eternal Tapestry," is not merely a historical overview but an exploration of the underlying threads that have woven together the fabric of Indian civilization.

A Land of Contrasts and Continuities

At first glance, India presents a paradox: it is both ancient and modern, traditional and dynamic, unified in its diversity while boasting a myriad of regional identities. This duality is at the core of what makes India so captivating. The country's story is one of contrasts—where ancient temples stand beside towering skyscrapers, and time-honored customs continue to coexist with rapid technological advancements. This juxtaposition is central to understanding how India has managed to maintain its rich cultural heritage despite undergoing profound social, political, and economic transformations.

In many ways, India's history is a narrative of synthesis. It has been a crucible of ideas and innovations, drawing influences from neighboring civilizations, welcoming invaders and traders, and eventually creating a unique mosaic that is distinctly Indian. The blending of indigenous traditions with external influences has resulted in a cultural tapestry that is both resilient and adaptive. As historians like John Keay have noted in *India: A History*, the subcontinent's ability to absorb and transform foreign elements is a testament to its deep-rooted pluralism and enduring spirit.

The Tapestry's Threads: Culture, Religion, and Philosophy

One of the most striking features of India is its cultural diversity, which finds its roots in the myriad religious and philosophical traditions that have flourished on the subcontinent. From the ancient Vedic traditions to the profound teachings of Buddhism, Jainism, and later, the devotional movements of Bhakti and Sufism, religion has been a defining factor in shaping Indian society. Each tradition has contributed its own unique threads to the overall tapestry.

For instance, the philosophical depth found in texts such as the *Upanishads* and later, works discussed by scholars like Romila Thapar in *Ancient India*, reveal a tradition that is both introspective and expansive. These texts delve into questions of existence, purpose, and the nature of reality—questions that continue to resonate with readers even today. This introspection is balanced by a vibrant culture of art, literature, and music, which has been celebrated across centuries.

Artistic expressions, whether in the form of classical dance, music, or literature, have also played a pivotal role in the formation of India's identity. The enduring appeal of epic narratives like the *Mahabharata* and the *Ramayana* lies not just in their storytelling but in their reflection of complex human emotions and societal values. These epics have influenced countless generations and remain integral to the cultural consciousness of India.

Historical Layers and the Passage of Time

India's history is not linear but a series of layers that have built upon one another. Each period, whether it be the ancient, medieval, or modern era, adds its own distinctive motif to the overall design. The subcontinent has witnessed the rise and fall of empires, the spread of revolutionary ideas, and the relentless pursuit of knowledge. This layering process gives India a sense of continuity despite the apparent ruptures and upheavals over the centuries.

Consider, for example, the Mauryan Empire under Ashoka, whose embrace of Buddhism after the Kalinga War signaled a significant shift in governance and philosophy. Ashoka's transformation and his subsequent efforts to propagate Buddhist teachings throughout Asia left an indelible mark on the region. The legacy of such transformative periods is echoed in later works, including Jawaharlal Nehru's *The Discovery of India*, which provides insights into how these ancient legacies continue to shape modern India.

Moreover, India's medieval period is characterized by a remarkable confluence of cultures. The arrival of Islam brought new art forms, administrative practices, and spiritual ideas that enriched the Indian milieu. The syncretic culture that emerged during the Mughal era is a prime example of India's capacity for cultural integration. Architectural marvels like the Taj Mahal stand as enduring symbols of this harmonious blend of traditions. Historians have long debated the nuances of this era, and works like those by Edward Luce in *In Spite of the Gods* offer compelling analyses of how these cultural intersections influenced India's socio-political landscape.

The Geography of Diversity

Geography has played a significant role in shaping India's history and cultural diversity. The subcontinent's varied landscapes—from the towering Himalayas in the north to the tropical regions of the south, from arid deserts in the west to the lush, fertile plains of the east—have influenced the development of distinct regional cultures. Each geographical zone has contributed its own traditions, cuisines, languages, and lifestyles, all of which add depth to India's historical narrative.

This geographical diversity has also contributed to the resilience of Indian civilization. The varied terrain has often provided natural fortifications against invasions and has allowed distinct cultural practices to flourish in relative isolation. Yet, the need to traverse these challenging landscapes also spurred advancements in technology, trade, and communication, thereby knitting the regions together. In his comprehensive works, scholars often highlight the interplay between geography and history as a crucial element in understanding the subcontinent's evolution.

The Enduring Impact of Colonial Encounters

While India's historical tapestry is ancient, it is impossible to discuss its evolution without addressing the profound impact of colonial encounters. The arrival of European traders and later, the establishment of British colonial rule, marked a turning point in the subcontinent's history. Colonialism brought with it both disruption and modernization. It reconfigured social structures, reoriented economic practices, and introduced new administrative systems. Yet, even as colonial powers attempted to reshape Indian society, the intrinsic strength of its cultural tapestry remained resilient.

The colonial period is a study in contrasts. On one hand, it led to the extraction of resources and significant cultural impositions; on the other, it ignited a powerful nationalist movement that sought to reclaim India's identity and independence. The struggle for freedom, as captured in various historical texts and biographies, is a testament to the indomitable spirit of the Indian people. This duality of destruction and renewal is a recurring theme throughout India's history, reminding us that even in the face of adversity, the underlying threads of cultural and historical identity endure.

The Narrative of Resilience and Renewal

What makes the study of India's history particularly compelling is its narrative of resilience and renewal. Despite facing numerous challenges—from natural calamities and foreign invasions to the internal strife and the impacts of colonialism—India has continually reinvented itself. Each phase of crisis has been followed by periods of renaissance, where innovation and cultural revival have taken center stage.

This cycle of decline and regeneration is not unique to India, but its scale and persistence over millennia are awe-inspiring. For example, following periods of turmoil during the medieval era, the resurgence of art and architecture during the Mughal period not only signified recovery but also a flowering of creativity that continues to influence contemporary culture. Such examples underscore the idea that the history of India is not just a record of events, but a living chronicle of human endeavor—a tapestry that is continuously woven, unraveled, and rewoven by the forces of time and circumstance.

Interconnections with Global History

An exploration of India's historical tapestry is incomplete without considering its global connections. From ancient trade routes that linked India to the Roman Empire, China, and the Middle East, to its modern role as a key player in international politics and economics, India has always been an integral part of the global narrative. The subcontinent's contributions to mathematics, science, philosophy, and literature have left an indelible mark on world civilization.

Books such as *India: A History* by John Keay offer readers a broader perspective on how India's interactions with other civilizations have enriched not only its own culture but also the global repository of knowledge. The intermingling of ideas across borders is a recurring motif in India's history—a theme that this book will explore in depth as we move through the centuries.

A Journey Through Time and Memory

As we begin this exploration of India's 2000-year journey, it is important to acknowledge that history is not just about dates and events; it is also about the stories, myths, and memories that define a people. Oral traditions, folk tales, and local legends have preserved the collective memory of communities, offering insights into the values, aspirations, and struggles of ordinary people. These narratives, often passed down through generations, are as much a part of India's historical record as the inscriptions on ancient monuments or the pages of classical texts.

In *The Discovery of India*, Jawaharlal Nehru reflects on the richness of these narratives and the importance of understanding history not merely as a sequence of events but as an evolving dialogue between the past and the present. The personal and the political, the mythic and the historical, are intertwined in ways that continue to shape the identity of India today.

Setting the Stage for the Journey Ahead

This book aims to provide a concise yet comprehensive history of India—a narrative that spans two millennia and captures the essence of a civilization that is both ancient and perpetually new. In the chapters that follow, we will delve into the various epochs that have defined India's past: from the flourishing of ancient empires and the rise of profound spiritual traditions to the dramatic transformations brought about by colonialism and the birth of a modern republic.

Each chapter will build on the themes introduced here, offering detailed accounts of the pivotal moments, influential figures, and transformative ideas that have guided India's evolution. By interweaving scholarly research with engaging narratives, this work aspires to be both a historical record and a tribute to the enduring spirit of India—a civilization that, despite countless challenges, continues to thrive and reinvent itself.

Concluding Thoughts

In reflecting on India's eternal tapestry, one is reminded of the words of eminent historians and thinkers who have grappled with the complexities of Indian identity. The layered narratives of conquest and conquest, tradition and innovation, strife and triumph, all come together to form a picture of a nation that is as multifaceted as it is unified. As we journey through the chapters ahead, let us keep in mind that the story of India is not just about rulers and battles, but about the everyday lives of millions whose experiences have contributed to a legacy of profound resilience and creativity.

This chapter has sought to lay the groundwork for understanding the myriad influences that have shaped India's destiny. It invites the reader to see beyond simplistic narratives and to appreciate the intricate, interwoven threads that form the rich tapestry of Indian history. In doing so, we honor the enduring spirit of a civilization that continues to captivate the imagination and inspire new generations around the world.

As you turn the page, prepare to embark on an odyssey that will traverse ancient river valleys, monumental empires, and modern metropolises—a journey that reveals the deep, pulsating heart of a land whose story is as eternal as the river Ganges itself. For further insights into these themes, readers may consult works like *India: A History* by John Keay, *The*

Discovery of India by Jawaharlal Nehru, and *Ancient India* by Romila Thapar, each of which offers unique perspectives that enrich our understanding of this vast and complex subject.

In essence, the narrative we begin here is not only a chronicle of events and eras but also a celebration of a living heritage—a tapestry that, despite its age, continues to evolve and inspire. Welcome to the beginning of India's eternal tapestry.

2

Dawn of Civilization – From the Indus to the Vedic Age

The story of India begins with a dawn of civilization that is as enigmatic as it is foundational. In this chapter, we explore the earliest chapters of Indian history—from the sophisticated urban centers of the Indus Valley Civilization to the emergence of the Vedic Age. These formative periods not only laid the groundwork for India's cultural and social fabric but also introduced ideas and practices that have echoed through millennia. In doing so, we delve into archaeological discoveries, ancient texts, and the works of modern historians who have pieced together a narrative that bridges myth and material culture.

The Indus Valley Civilization: Cradle of Urban Ingenuity

The Indus Valley Civilization (circa 3300–1300 BCE) is among the world's earliest urban societies. Flourishing along the fertile floodplains of the Indus River and its tributaries, this civilization is celebrated for its planned cities, advanced drainage systems, and a mysterious script that has yet to be fully deciphered. Cities like Harappa, Mohenjo-Daro, and Dholavira reveal a society that was remarkably organized and sophisticated.

Urban Planning and Technological Prowess

One of the most striking features of the Indus cities is their urban planning. Archaeological evidence indicates that these cities were laid out on grid patterns, with wide streets, public buildings, and intricate drainage systems that suggest a high degree of civic organization. The uniformity of brick sizes and weights used in construction implies standardized production methods, hinting at a centralized administrative structure. Scholars such as Gregory L. Possehl, in his seminal work *The Indus Civilization: A Contemporary Perspective*, argue that these features point to a well-organized state system that was uniquely advanced for its time.

Economic and Social Life

Economic activities during this period were diverse, encompassing agriculture, trade, and artisanal production. The presence of standardized weights and measures indicates that trade was both local and long-distance, linking the Indus Valley to distant regions through robust commercial networks. The discovery of seals and inscriptions also suggests that the civilization had established systems of record-keeping and possibly even early forms of writing. Socially, the uniformity in housing and artifacts across sites points to a society that was relatively egalitarian, though the precise nature of social stratification remains a topic of debate among historians.

Cultural and Religious Practices

The religious life of the Indus people is inferred from various artifacts, such as figurines, terracotta statues, and what some scholars believe to be early representations of deities. Although the precise nature of their beliefs remains shrouded in mystery, there is evidence to suggest that the seeds of later Hindu practices—such as the worship of mother goddesses and the veneration of natural elements—may have been present during this period. Works like *The Indus Saga* by Shereen Ratnagar explore these connections, proposing that the cultural practices of the Indus Valley laid the early foundations for the later spiritual traditions of India.

Transition to the Vedic Age: Emergence of New Ideals

Following the decline of the urban centers of the Indus Valley Civilization, India experienced a transformation that led to the rise of what is now known as the Vedic Age (circa 1500–500 BCE). This period is characterized by the migration of Indo-Aryan peoples into the subcontinent, a movement that brought profound changes in social structure, religious practice, and linguistic expression.

The Arrival of the Indo-Aryans

The migration of the Indo-Aryans is one of the most debated topics in Indian historiography. According to linguistic and archaeological evidence, these groups brought with them a new language—the precursor to Sanskrit—and a collection of texts that would come to be known as the Vedas. The Rigveda, the oldest of these texts, not only provides insight into the religious and philosophical world of the early Indo-Aryans but also offers glimpses into their social organization and rituals. In *Ancient India*, Romila Thapar discusses how the Rigvedic hymns reflect a society in transition—from one that was organized around the remnants of the urban traditions of the Indus Valley to one that was increasingly pastoral and tribal in nature.

Society and Social Structures

The social landscape of the Vedic Age was markedly different from that of the urban Indus cities. Rather than large, centralized urban centers, the Vedic period was characterized by smaller, more dispersed communities and a tribal system organized around kinship groups. The early Vedic society appears to have been relatively egalitarian, though later texts hint at the emergence of social stratification. The evolution of the varna system, which eventually crystallized into a rigid caste structure, began during this period as roles and responsibilities within the community became more specialized. This gradual differentiation of society is a topic explored in depth in *The Discovery of India* by Jawaharlal Nehru, where the author reflects on how these early developments set the stage for centuries of social and cultural evolution.

Religious and Philosophical Developments

Religion during the Vedic Age underwent a significant transformation. The early Vedic rituals, which centered on the performance of elaborate sacrifices to appease various deities, gradually evolved into more philosophical inquiries about the nature of existence. The latter Vedic texts, known as the Upanishads, marked a turning point by introducing abstract concepts such as Brahman (the ultimate reality) and Atman (the inner self). These ideas laid the philosophical groundwork for later schools of thought in Hinduism, including Vedanta and various forms of mysticism. Scholars such as Wendy Doniger have noted that the Upanishads represent one of the earliest recorded forays into philosophical inquiry in human history, making them crucial not only to Indian thought but also to the broader narrative of world philosophy.

Synthesis of Material Culture and Spiritual Thought

The transition from the urban sophistication of the Indus Valley to the more dispersed, ritualistic society of the Vedic Age is marked by a synthesis of material and spiritual elements that has defined Indian civilization. In the cities of the Indus Valley, the focus was on practical innovations such as urban planning, metallurgy, and trade. By contrast, the Vedic period witnessed an increasing emphasis on ritual, poetry, and philosophy. This duality reflects a broader trend in Indian history, where technological and artistic achievements are often interwoven with profound spiritual insights.

Art and Literature

Although the Vedic period is primarily remembered for its religious texts and hymns, it also saw the emergence of early literary traditions. The oral transmission of the Vedas was an art form in itself, relying on precise memorization and recitation techniques that ensured the survival of these texts over generations. This method of preservation and the poetic beauty of the hymns have been celebrated by scholars and poets alike. In *India: A History*, John Keay emphasizes how these early literary forms not only served a religious purpose but also laid the foundation for a rich tradition of storytelling and intellectual inquiry that would flourish in later centuries.

The Role of Rituals and Sacrifices

Rituals played a central role in the daily life of the Vedic people. The performance of yajnas (sacrificial rituals) was seen as a means of maintaining cosmic order and ensuring the prosperity of the community. These rituals were intricately connected to the natural cycles of life and the seasons, reflecting an intimate relationship between the people and their environment. The meticulous nature of these practices suggests a deep understanding of both the material and spiritual worlds. Historians like Michael Witzel have argued that the ritualistic practices of the Vedic age were not only religious acts but also served as a means of social cohesion, reinforcing the bonds within the community while also delineating the roles and responsibilities of its members.

Bridging Myth and Reality

One of the enduring challenges in studying the early history of India is the interplay between myth and historical fact. The Vedic texts, while invaluable for understanding the period, are imbued with symbolic language and mythological narratives that require careful interpretation. The legends of gods, heroes, and cosmic battles found in these texts have often been seen as allegorical, representing deeper truths about the human condition and the nature of the universe. Scholars such as Alf Hiltebeitel, in his analysis of myth and ritual in early India, argue that these stories are not to be dismissed as mere fables but must be understood as powerful expressions of the cultural and spiritual psyche of the time.

Archaeological Insights and Textual Analysis

Modern archaeology has played a critical role in shedding light on the transition from the Indus Valley Civilization to the Vedic Age. Excavations at sites across northwestern India have unearthed artifacts that suggest continuity in certain aspects of material culture, even as the predominant way of life shifted. These findings support the view that the arrival of the Indo-Aryans did not represent a complete break with the past but rather a process of cultural transformation. This synthesis of new and old is a theme that recurs throughout Indian history and is vividly captured in the interdisciplinary studies that combine archaeological data with textual analysis. In works like *Ancient India*, Romila Thapar highlights how this confluence of evidence from different sources enriches our understanding of the period.

Reflections on Legacy and Continuity

The legacy of the Indus and Vedic periods is profound and far-reaching. The technological advancements and urban innovations of the Indus Valley set standards for civic organization that would influence later civilizations. At the same time, the spiritual and philosophical insights of the Vedic Age provided a cultural and intellectual framework that continues to resonate in modern India. The dialogue between material achievements and spiritual inquiry established during these formative periods remains a defining feature of Indian civilization.

Impact on Later Historical Developments

The ideas and practices that emerged during these early periods have been transmitted, transformed, and reinterpreted over the centuries. The social structures that began to take shape in the Vedic period would eventually evolve into the complex caste system, while the philosophical concepts introduced in the Upanishads became the cornerstone of later Hindu thought. This dual legacy of practical innovation and intellectual depth is a recurring motif in Indian history, as noted by Jawaharlal Nehru in *The Discovery of India*, where he reflects on how these early contributions continue to shape India's modern identity.

A Living Heritage

Today, the influence of these ancient periods can be seen in everything from the layout of modern cities to the enduring relevance of religious rituals and philosophical debates. The echoes of the Indus Valley's urban sophistication are visible in India's emphasis on organized planning and community life, while the contemplative spirit of the Vedic Age lives on in the country's vibrant intellectual and spiritual traditions. This living heritage is a testament to the resilience and adaptability of Indian civilization—a civilization that has continually reinterpreted its past to navigate the challenges of the present and future.

Concluding Thoughts

The journey from the Indus Valley Civilization to the Vedic Age represents not merely a chronological progression but a profound transformation in the ways people organized their lives, expressed their beliefs, and related to one another. It is a period marked by both continuity and change—a time when the seeds of India's rich cultural, technological, and spiritual traditions were sown.

By examining the urban marvels of Harappa and Mohenjo-Daro alongside the poetic meditations of the Rigveda and Upanishads, we gain insight into a complex tapestry where practical ingenuity and metaphysical inquiry are interwoven. As modern historians continue to debate and reinterpret these early chapters, works like Gregory L. Possehl's *The Indus Civilization: A Contemporary Perspective*, Romila Thapar's *Ancient India*, and John Keay's *India: A History* remain invaluable resources, offering multiple lenses through which to view this dynamic past.

The narrative of India's dawn is one of transformation—a story where an ancient civilization's decline gave rise to new cultural expressions and where indigenous innovations blended with migrating traditions to create a legacy that is as enduring as it is influential. In the face of ongoing debates and new discoveries, our understanding of this period continues to evolve, reminding us that history is not static but a living conversation between the past and the present.

In closing, the early chapters of India's history invite us to reflect on the interplay between civilization and culture, between tangible innovations and intangible ideas. They prompt us to appreciate not only the achievements of our ancestors but also the transformative processes that continue to shape modern India. As we move forward in this exploration, we carry with us the lessons of the Indus and Vedic eras—lessons of resilience, creativity, and the enduring human quest for meaning and order in a changing world.

The dawn of civilization in India, with its blend of urban planning, ritualistic innovation, and philosophical exploration, remains a cornerstone of the subcontinent's identity. It is a period that challenges our assumptions about progress and invites us to see history as a series of layered, interconnected narratives—a vibrant mosaic that continues to inform and inspire.

3

Empires of Antiquity – Maurya and Gupta Dynasties

In the sweeping panorama of Indian history, few periods shine as brightly as the age of great empires whose vision and achievements laid the foundations for the cultural, political, and economic framework of the subcontinent. This chapter explores two such remarkable epochs—the Maurya and Gupta dynasties—each representing a pinnacle of statecraft, intellectual inquiry, and cultural efflorescence that has resonated through the ages.

The Maurya Empire: Unity and Transformation

Founding and Expansion

The Maurya Empire, founded in the late 4th century BCE by Chandragupta Maurya, represents one of the earliest attempts at unifying the vast and diverse regions of India under a single political authority. Emerging in the wake of Alexander the Great's incursions into northwest India, the Mauryan state capitalized on a climate of regional turbulence. Chandragupta's vision of a unified realm was realized through both military conquest and sophisticated administrative strategies. His efforts established the blueprint for statecraft in India, one that was later expanded by his successors.

Historians such as Romila Thapar, in her work *Ancient India*, argue that Chandragupta's success was not merely due to martial prowess but also to the adoption of an efficient bureaucratic system that facilitated governance across a sprawling territory. This model, blending military organization with a centralized administrative mechanism, set the stage for one of the most influential empires in Indian history.

Ashoka and the Transformation of Governance

Perhaps the most celebrated figure of the Mauryan era is Emperor Ashoka, whose reign (268–232 BCE) transformed the empire and left an indelible mark on the subcontinent and beyond. Ashoka's conversion to Buddhism after the bloody Kalinga War initiated a radical shift in policy—from conquest to compassion, from expansionism to the propagation of ethical governance. His edicts, inscribed on pillars and rock faces throughout his realm, emphasize moral virtues such as non-violence (ahimsa), tolerance, and justice.

In his acclaimed work *Ashoka: The Search for India's Lost Emperor*, Charles Allen explores how Ashoka's policies not only reformed the administration but also sowed the seeds for the spread of Buddhism across Asia. Ashoka's edicts serve as early examples of state-sponsored social reform, and they have been pivotal in framing India's ethical and cultural legacy. His embrace of Buddhism as a unifying ideology helped bridge the diverse religious practices within the empire, promoting a vision of universal brotherhood and shared human values.

Administrative Innovations and Socio-Economic Developments

Under Mauryan rule, the structure of governance was characterized by meticulous organization. A network of provincial administrators, spies, and officials worked together to ensure that the edicts of the emperor were implemented throughout the empire. This administrative model provided stability, allowing for economic prosperity, extensive trade, and infrastructural development. The construction of roads, irrigation systems, and public works projects not only improved the quality of life for ordinary citizens but also facilitated the movement of armies and goods, contributing to the empire's cohesion.

Economic prosperity under the Mauryas was further bolstered by a system of standardized coinage, trade routes, and market regulation. These policies laid the groundwork for a robust economic framework that would later be expanded and refined by succeeding dynasties. Scholars such as John Keay, in *India: A History*, emphasize that the Mauryan period set a precedent for state-driven economic and infrastructural development, highlighting the empire's enduring impact on later periods.

The Gupta Empire: A Golden Age of Culture and Learning

The Rise of the Gupta Dynasty

Following centuries of political fragmentation after the Mauryan decline, India witnessed the emergence of another transformative empire—the Gupta dynasty, which ruled from approximately 320 to 550 CE. Often referred to as the "Golden Age" of India, the Gupta period is celebrated for its advancements in science, mathematics, literature, and the arts. Under the leadership of rulers like Chandragupta I, Samudragupta, and Chandragupta II, the Gupta Empire not only reasserted political unity but also became a center for cultural and intellectual achievement.

The rise of the Gupta Empire marked a period of relative stability and prosperity, which allowed arts and learning to flourish. In *The Wonder That Was India*, historian A.L. Basham details how the Gupta rulers fostered an environment where literature, art, and scientific inquiry were given unprecedented patronage. The stability of Gupta rule provided fertile ground for innovation, setting in motion developments that would influence both India and the wider world for centuries.

Cultural Renaissance and Intellectual Flourishing

One of the most compelling aspects of the Gupta period was its unparalleled cultural renaissance. Art and literature experienced a surge of creativity, with intricate sculptures, elegant cave temples, and exquisite coins that continue to be admired for their aesthetic beauty. The Gupta style of art, characterized by idealized depictions of deities and human forms, represented a synthesis of spiritual devotion and naturalistic expression. These artistic achievements have had a lasting legacy, influencing subsequent artistic traditions not only in India but also in regions as far-flung as Southeast Asia.

In literature, the Gupta age witnessed the composition of enduring works in Sanskrit, the refined literary language that became a vehicle for both poetry and scholarly treatises. Kalidasa, often regarded as India's greatest poet and dramatist, flourished during this period. His plays and poems, including the renowned *Shakuntala*, encapsulate the refined sensibilities and philosophical depth that characterized Gupta culture. These works continue to be celebrated for their linguistic elegance and profound insights into human nature.

Scientific and Mathematical Innovations

The Gupta period was also a time of significant scientific and mathematical advancements. Mathematicians such as Aryabhata made groundbreaking contributions that would shape the future of science. Aryabhata's work on the concept of zero, place value, and the approximation of π (pi) was revolutionary, marking a pivotal moment in the evolution of mathematical thought. His treatise, *Aryabhatiya*, remains a landmark in the history of mathematics and astronomy, highlighting the sophisticated level of intellectual inquiry during the Gupta era.

The Gupta scholars were not limited to mathematics alone; they also made substantial strides in medicine, astronomy, and metallurgy. Their scientific endeavors were deeply intertwined with philosophical and spiritual explorations, reflecting a worldview where the empirical and the mystical coexisted harmoniously. The integration of science and spirituality during this time provided a model for holistic inquiry—a theme that resonates with the broader tapestry of Indian intellectual history.

Administration and Economic Prosperity

Parallel to their cultural and scientific achievements, the Guptas instituted a well-structured administrative system that contributed to the empire's longevity. The decentralization of power allowed for greater local autonomy, while still maintaining the overarching authority of the Gupta rulers. This system promoted efficient governance, bolstered economic activity, and supported a network of trade that extended to the Mediterranean, Southeast Asia, and beyond.

Economic prosperity during the Gupta era was evident in the flourishing of agriculture, handicrafts, and trade. The period saw the development of urban centers that became hubs of commercial and cultural activity. Markets teemed with goods ranging from textiles and spices to precious metals and art. This economic dynamism, supported by stable governance and infrastructural investments, created a society in which art, science, and literature could thrive in tandem.

Comparative Reflections and Enduring Legacies

Convergence of Military Might and Cultural Patronage

Both the Maurya and Gupta empires exemplify the dynamic interplay between military power and cultural patronage—a combination that proved instrumental in shaping India's historical trajectory. While the Mauryas are remembered for their expansive territorial conquests and transformative governance, the Guptas are celebrated for ushering in a golden age of cultural and intellectual achievements. This dual legacy is significant because it underscores how statecraft in India has historically been a balanced act—one that values both order and creativity.

Historians like Romila Thapar and John Keay have often emphasized that the achievements of these empires were not merely the result of strong leadership but also of an integrated approach to governance that nurtured cultural and intellectual life. In *The Discovery of India*, Jawaharlal Nehru reflects on how the legacy of these great empires continues to influence modern India, serving as a reminder of the nation's potential to combine pragmatic administration with artistic and scientific innovation.

Interconnections and Influence Beyond Borders

The influence of the Maurya and Gupta empires extended far beyond the borders of India. The spread of Buddhism under Ashoka's patronage, for example, helped establish India as a cultural and religious hub in Asia. Buddhist ideas and practices disseminated along the Silk Road and into East Asia, leaving a profound impact on the spiritual landscape of regions such as China, Korea, and Japan. Similarly, the scientific and mathematical innovations of the Gupta period influenced scholars in the Islamic world and later in medieval Europe, underscoring the global relevance of India's intellectual contributions.

These interconnections highlight a historical pattern where Indian thought and governance transcended local boundaries, contributing to a broader tapestry of human achievement. Works like Charles Allen's *Ashoka: The Search for India's Lost Emperor* provide vivid narratives of how the Mauryan legacy resonated across continents, while A.L. Basham's *The Wonder*

That Was India contextualizes the far-reaching impact of Gupta innovations in art, literature, and science.

Concluding Thoughts

The Maurya and Gupta empires stand as monumental testaments to the enduring power of visionary leadership and integrated statecraft. From Chandragupta's unification of diverse territories to Ashoka's ethical reforms and the Guptas' golden age of cultural and scientific flourishing, these periods have left an indelible legacy on the history of India. Their achievements illustrate how a civilization can harness military might, administrative ingenuity, and cultural patronage to create a society that is both orderly and imaginative—a society that continues to inspire future generations.

In tracing the development of these empires, we are reminded of the importance of balancing power with compassion, innovation with tradition, and pragmatism with artistic expression. The legacy of these ancient dynasties offers valuable lessons for modern India and the world, emphasizing that sustainable progress arises from the harmonious integration of diverse human pursuits.

As we reflect on the achievements of the Maurya and Gupta periods, it becomes evident that their influence is woven into the very fabric of India's identity. Their contributions to governance, culture, and intellectual thought have not only defined historical trajectories but continue to shape the aspirations and values of contemporary society. For readers seeking deeper insights into these epochs, works such as Romila Thapar's *Ancient India*, John Keay's *India: A History*, and Jawaharlal Nehru's *The Discovery of India* provide rich, nuanced accounts that complement and enhance our understanding of this transformative era.

In the grand narrative of India's history, the Maurya and Gupta empires emerge as vibrant chapters—each a distinct yet interlinked expression of a civilization's quest for unity, knowledge, and beauty. As we move forward in this exploration of India's past, let us carry forward the lessons of these empires, recognizing that the interplay of power, culture, and intellect remains as relevant today as it was two millennia ago.

The story of these empires is not just one of conquests and courtly grandeur; it is a story of ideas that have transcended time—a story of moral evolution, scientific breakthroughs, and artistic achievements that continue to illuminate the path of human progress. In celebrating the legacy of the Maurya and Gupta dynasties, we honor a tradition of excellence that has helped shape the contours of Indian civilization, offering a source of inspiration for generations to come.

In essence, the era of the Mauryas and the Guptas invites us to witness the convergence of military valor and intellectual brilliance—a confluence that has rendered India's past both formidable and fascinating. Their achievements, encapsulated in the visionary reforms of Ashoka and the cultural renaissance of the Gupta period, remain a beacon of hope and possibility, urging us to imagine a future that is informed by the wisdom of our ancestors.

4

Medieval Mosaic – Kingdoms, Invasions, and Syncretism

Medieval India presents a rich mosaic of political entities, cultural exchanges, and transformative encounters. This chapter explores a period marked by regional kingdoms, successive invasions, and an emerging syncretism that reshaped the subcontinent's social, cultural, and religious landscapes. Over the course of several centuries, India experienced a profound transformation as indigenous traditions met and merged with influences from Central Asia, the Middle East, and beyond. The resulting tapestry of medieval India is one of both conflict and convergence—a complex interplay of conquest and cultural synthesis.

The Landscape of Medieval Kingdoms

The Fragmented Political Terrain

After the decline of the classical empires, India entered a phase of political fragmentation. The large centralized states of the Maurya and Gupta eras gave way to numerous regional kingdoms. In the northern and central parts of India, powerful dynasties such as the Pratiharas, Palas, and Rashtrakutas vied for supremacy, while the south witnessed the rise of the Chalukyas, Cholas, and later, the Vijayanagara Empire. This era was characterized by a decentralized political order where local rulers maintained considerable autonomy.

Historians like Satish Chandra, in *Medieval India: From Sultanat to the Mughals*, argue that this fragmentation was not merely a decline but also a period of vibrant regional expression. Local dynasties developed their own administrative systems, art forms, and cultural practices, all the while engaging in both conflict and cooperation with neighboring states. These kingdoms provided the fertile ground for the blossoming of regional literature, temple architecture, and a unique synthesis of indigenous practices with external influences.

Administrative Innovations and Local Governance

Many of these kingdoms implemented sophisticated administrative structures that were adapted to their local needs. For example, the Cholas are renowned for their efficient system of local governance, which integrated village assemblies and decentralized revenue collection. This model enabled them to maintain control over vast territories despite the absence of a strong central bureaucracy. Such systems, documented in works like *The Age of Temples in India* by James Burgess, demonstrate that even in a fragmented political landscape, innovation in administration was thriving.

These local governance systems were not isolated; they frequently interacted with each other through alliances, marriages, and trade, creating a network of interdependent polities. This connectivity laid the foundation for the cross-cultural exchanges that would come to define the medieval period.

Waves of Invasion and the Transformation of the Political Order

Early Invasions and the Impact on Indian Polity

The medieval period was also marked by a series of invasions that brought profound changes to India's political and cultural milieu. Beginning with incursions from the northwest, the subcontinent was exposed to the armies of Central Asia and the Islamic world. These early invasions, while initially limited in their scope, set the stage for more sustained campaigns in later centuries.

One of the most significant invasions came with the arrival of Muhammad of Ghor in the late 12th century. His conquests led to the establishment of the Delhi Sultanate, a series of dynasties that would rule large parts of northern India for several centuries. In *The Delhi Sultanate: A Political and Military History*, Peter Jackson outlines how these invasions not only disrupted established political structures but also introduced new administrative practices, art forms, and religious ideas that would leave an enduring mark on the region.

The Delhi Sultanate: A New Political Order

The establishment of the Delhi Sultanate represented a turning point in medieval Indian history. Under the rule of dynasties such as the Mamluks, Khiljis, Tughlaqs, and Lodis, the Sultanate imposed a centralized system that differed markedly from the decentralized governance of earlier regional kingdoms. The Sultanate's rulers were adept at integrating military conquest with administrative reform. They introduced new revenue systems, such as the iqta system, which allocated land revenue rights to military officers and administrators in lieu of direct taxation. This approach not only consolidated their power but also allowed for a degree of local autonomy, as traditional rulers were often co-opted into the new system.

The influx of Muslim administrators, scholars, and artisans transformed the cultural landscape of northern India. The architectural legacy of the Sultanate is visible in the construction of grand mosques, forts, and mausoleums. Iconic structures such as the Qutb Minar in Delhi testify to a period of ambitious architectural innovation. Historians like Richard Eaton, in *The Rise of Islam and the Bengal Frontier, 1204–1760*, highlight that the Delhi Sultanate was not solely a period of conflict but also one of significant cultural transformation, as Muslim and indigenous traditions began to intermingle.

Syncretism: The Confluence of Cultures

The Fusion of Religious Traditions

Perhaps the most enduring legacy of medieval India is the syncretic blending of cultures and religious practices. As Muslim rulers and indigenous communities interacted over centuries, a unique cultural synthesis emerged—one that defied simplistic binaries of "Islamic" versus "Hindu." This period saw the emergence of a new spiritual ethos that combined elements of Sufism with Bhakti traditions. Sufi saints, with their emphasis on personal devotion, mysticism, and the universality of love, found a receptive audience among Hindu communities. Similarly, Bhakti poets and philosophers, who emphasized the internal experience of the divine over ritualistic practice, began to incorporate elements from Islamic mysticism into their teachings.

Works like *The Sufi Saints of India* by Carl W. Ernst and *Bhakti and Sufism: A Conversation* edited by Ziauddin Sardar explore this intermingling in depth. These syncretic movements were not only spiritual in nature but also had a profound social impact. They challenged rigid social hierarchies and provided alternative models of community and devotion that transcended caste and creed. In many ways, the synthesis of Sufi and Bhakti traditions became a symbol of medieval India's pluralistic identity—a legacy that continues to influence contemporary cultural and religious discourse.

Artistic and Architectural Synthesis

The fusion of cultural influences during the medieval period was vividly expressed in the art and architecture of the time. The architectural styles developed under the Delhi Sultanate, for example, are characterized by a blend of Islamic motifs with indigenous craftsmanship. The use of intricate calligraphy, geometric patterns, and the incorporation of traditional Indian decorative elements created a unique visual language that was both novel and deeply rooted in local traditions.

This architectural synthesis reached its zenith during the later stages of the Sultanate and into the early Mughal period. Monuments such as the Alai Darwaza and the Tughlaqabad Fort exemplify this blend of styles. The development of Indo-Islamic architecture is discussed in detail in *Indian Architecture (Buddhist and Hindu Period)* by Percy Brown, where the author traces the evolution of architectural forms as they absorbed influences from invading cultures while retaining core indigenous elements.

Literary and Cultural Cross-Pollination

Medieval India was also a period of rich literary production, where languages such as Persian, Sanskrit, and regional vernaculars flourished side by side. Courtly literature often reflected the multicultural realities of the time. Persian became the language of administration and high culture under the Sultanate, while local languages continued to thrive in poetry, folklore, and drama. This literary cross-pollination produced works that celebrated both the martial valor of rulers and the devotional mysticism of the common people.

The renowned poet Amir Khusrau, often hailed as the "Parrot of India," is a prime example of this syncretism. His compositions in Persian and Hindavi bridged the gap between the ruling elites and the local populace, enriching the cultural fabric of the time. Khusrau's works, which are examined in *The Legacy of Amir Khusrau* by Ananya Vajpeyi, encapsulate the spirit of medieval India—a blend of erudition, innovation, and deep humanism that transcended religious and cultural divides.

The Dynamics of Invasion and Indigenous Response

Resistance and Adaptation

While invasions brought about significant cultural and administrative changes, they also met with resistance from indigenous powers. Many local rulers fought fiercely to preserve their traditions and autonomy, even as they had to adapt to the new political realities. The Rajput kingdoms, for example, are well-known for their martial prowess and staunch defense of their territories. Their resistance against repeated invasions from the north is a testament to the resilience of indigenous political and cultural identities.

Historians such as K. S. Lal, in *The Mughal Harem*, discuss how these indigenous responses were not merely reactions to foreign dominance but also initiatives to redefine identity in a changing world. The Rajputs, along with other regional powers, negotiated a complex relationship with the invaders—sometimes allying with them, at other times engaging in open conflict. This dynamic interplay between resistance and adaptation contributed to the emergence of a pluralistic society, where multiple narratives coexisted and influenced one another.

The Role of Trade and Urban Centers

In addition to military and political changes, the medieval period was marked by the growth of urban centers and thriving trade networks. Cities like Delhi, Agra, and Hyderabad became melting pots of cultural and economic activity. These urban centers were not only administrative capitals but also hubs where artisans, traders, scholars, and religious leaders converged. The resulting interactions accelerated the flow of ideas, goods, and technologies, further enriching the cultural milieu.

The economic dynamism of this period is well documented in works such as *Commerce and Culture in Indian History* by Irfan Habib. Habib argues that the robust trade networks and urban growth during the medieval era facilitated cultural exchanges that transcended regional boundaries. Markets became spaces of dialogue where diverse traditions merged, laying the groundwork for a syncretic culture that was uniquely Indian.

Reflections on the Medieval Legacy

A Mosaic of Pluralism and Innovation

Medieval India, with its ever-shifting political alliances, waves of invasion, and rich tapestry of cultural syncretism, offers a compelling narrative of transformation. The period was defined not by uniformity, but by the coexistence of multiple cultural, political, and religious traditions. This pluralism—borne out of both conflict and cooperation—became one of the defining features of Indian civilization. It is a legacy that continues to resonate in modern India, where diversity is celebrated as a source of strength and creativity.

The synthesis of diverse traditions during the medieval period has been a subject of fascination for scholars across disciplines. In *Medieval India: A History*, Satish Chandra eloquently outlines how the interplay between invading forces and indigenous traditions resulted in a hybrid culture that was dynamic, resilient, and profoundly innovative. This period, with its mix of martial valor and cultural patronage, stands as a testament to the enduring capacity of Indian society to adapt and transform in the face of change.

Enduring Influences on Contemporary India

The impact of the medieval mosaic is evident in contemporary India in numerous ways. Modern Indian art, literature, music, and even administrative practices bear the imprint of a period when cross-cultural exchanges reshaped the subcontinent's identity. The architectural legacies of the Delhi Sultanate and subsequent Indo-Islamic influences can be seen in many of India's iconic monuments, while the syncretic religious traditions that emerged during this era continue to inform the nation's spiritual landscape.

In *The Wonder That Was India*, A.L. Basham highlights how the cultural confluences of the medieval period have left an indelible mark on Indian society, underscoring the importance of historical pluralism as a foundation for modern democratic values. The enduring legacy of medieval syncretism is not merely a relic of the past; it is a living, evolving force that continues to inspire dialogue and creativity in contemporary cultural and social spheres.

Concluding Thoughts

Medieval India was a period of profound complexity—a time when kingdoms rose and fell, when foreign invaders left their mark, and when indigenous cultures engaged in a dynamic dance of conflict and convergence. The interplay of military might, administrative innovation, and cultural synthesis during this period created a legacy that is as multifaceted as it is enduring. The diverse political entities and the rich tapestry of syncretic traditions that emerged during these centuries offer valuable lessons about the power of pluralism and the capacity of human societies to transform and adapt.

As we reflect on this medieval mosaic, it becomes clear that the period's legacy is not defined solely by the narratives of conquest or resistance, but by the creative dialogue that emerged from these encounters. It is a reminder that history is not a single, linear story, but a confluence of multiple voices, traditions, and innovations—each contributing to the overall tapestry of human civilization.

For those interested in delving deeper into this transformative era, works such as Satish Chandra's *Medieval India: From Sultanat to the Mughals*, Peter Jackson's *The Delhi Sultanate: A Political and Military History*, and Richard Eaton's *The Rise of Islam and the Bengal Frontier, 1204–1760* offer rich insights and compelling narratives that further illuminate the intricate interplay of forces that shaped medieval India.

In closing, this chapter has sought to capture the essence of a period that was as turbulent as it was creative. The legacy of medieval India, with its kingdoms, invasions, and remarkable syncretism, remains a testament to the enduring spirit of a civilization that has continually reinvented itself in the face of change. This mosaic of diverse influences, challenges, and innovations not only defined an era but also laid the groundwork for the vibrant, pluralistic society that India is today.

The story of medieval India, therefore, is not just one of historical events—it is a story of resilience, transformation, and the eternal dialogue between the past and the present. As we move forward in our exploration of India's history, the lessons of this period remind us of the enduring power of cultural synthesis and the unyielding capacity of human societies to evolve and thrive through the interplay of diversity and unity.

5

The Mughal Legacy – Art, Architecture, and Administration

Few eras in Indian history have left as indelible a mark on the nation's cultural, artistic, and administrative landscapes as the Mughal period. Spanning from the early 16th to the mid-18th century, the Mughal era is renowned for its grandeur, innovation, and synthesis of diverse traditions. This chapter explores how the Mughals transformed India through a blend of centralized governance, sophisticated art and architecture, and cultural patronage that continues to shape the subcontinent's identity.

The Foundation of the Mughal Empire

Establishment and Expansion

The Mughal Empire was established by Babur in 1526 after his decisive victory over Ibrahim Lodi at the Battle of Panipat. Babur's entry into India was not just a military conquest; it was the beginning of an era that would redefine Indian society. His successors, notably Humayun, Akbar, Jahangir, Shah Jahan, and Aurangzeb, expanded and consolidated Mughal rule over vast territories, laying the groundwork for a centralized administrative system that integrated diverse peoples and traditions.

Babur's memoirs, *Baburnama*, offer a vivid account of the early challenges and aspirations of the Mughal enterprise. They reveal a leader who was as much a poet and chronicler as a conqueror—a figure determined to merge the splendor of Central Asian culture with the rich traditions of India. Historians such as Abraham Eraly, in *The Mughal Throne: The Saga of India's Great Emperors*, argue that the success of the Mughals was due to their ability to adapt to local contexts, forging alliances with regional powers and absorbing indigenous practices into their governance model.

A Policy of Inclusion

One of the most distinctive aspects of Mughal rule was its policy of inclusion. Akbar the Great, in particular, is celebrated for his efforts to build a syncretic empire that respected the plurality of Indian society. His administration integrated Hindus, Muslims, and people of other faiths through reforms such as the abolition of discriminatory taxes like the jizya and the establishment of a new, merit-based bureaucracy. Akbar's court became a center of intellectual and artistic activity, where scholars and poets from various backgrounds collaborated and exchanged ideas.

Akbar's policies are extensively discussed in *The Akbarnama* and later analyses such as Irfan Habib's *The Agrarian System of Mughal India*, which detail how his inclusive approach helped stabilize the empire and foster a culture of tolerance and innovation. This era of enlightened governance not only promoted administrative efficiency but also set a precedent for cultural synthesis that would define Mughal artistry and literature.

The Blossoming of Mughal Art and Architecture

Architectural Innovations and Iconic Structures

Mughal architecture is perhaps the most enduring symbol of their legacy. The Mughals brought together elements of Persian, Central Asian, and indigenous Indian design to create a style that was both majestic and uniquely suited to the Indian climate and culture. Structures like the Red Fort in Delhi, Humayun's Tomb in Agra, and the Taj Mahal are masterpieces that exemplify the Mughal synthesis of aesthetics, engineering, and symbolism.

The Taj Mahal, built by Shah Jahan as a monument to love, stands as a crowning achievement of Mughal architecture. Its harmonious proportions, intricate inlay work with precious stones, and the use of white marble have inspired architects around the world. Architectural historian Ebba Koch, in her work *The Complete Taj Mahal*, emphasizes how the monument reflects not only technical mastery but also a deep cultural and emotional resonance, capturing the essence of Mughal ideals of beauty and permanence.

Humayun's Tomb, another architectural marvel, represents the beginning of a tradition of monumental tomb architecture that influenced later structures. Its design, which features a central dome, surrounding gardens, and a careful balance of symmetry and spatial organization, set the template for subsequent Mughal edifices. Scholars such as Catherine Asher, in *Mughal Architecture: An Outline of Its History and Development*, note that these monuments are a testament to the Mughals' ability to fuse functional requirements with artistic expression, creating structures that continue to captivate the modern imagination.

A Flourishing of the Arts

The Mughal era was also a period of unparalleled artistic innovation. Miniature painting, a refined art form that flourished under Mughal patronage, combined vibrant colors, detailed naturalistic depictions, and intricate calligraphy to capture the grandeur of the court, the beauty of the natural world, and scenes from literature and daily life. The Mughal miniatures from Akbar's court, for instance, are celebrated for their exquisite detail and their ability to blend Persian artistic traditions with local Indian elements.

The synthesis of art and literature reached new heights during the reigns of Jahangir and Shah Jahan. Jahangir's love for nature and his keen eye for detail are evident in his commissioned paintings, which depict everything from lush landscapes to the delicate features of courtly figures. His memoirs, along with contemporary accounts, illustrate how art was used as a tool for both political propaganda and personal expression. Historians such as Milo C. Beach in *The Mughal Empire* highlight that Mughal art was more than decoration; it was a reflection of the emperor's vision of a harmonious, multicultural empire.

Literary patronage also played a crucial role in the cultural landscape of the Mughal court. Akbar's court, for example, was home to scholars, poets, and historians who wrote in multiple languages, including Persian, Sanskrit, and regional dialects. The resulting literature provided insights into the administrative, social, and philosophical dimensions of the empire. Works such as Abul Fazl's *Akbarnama* not only document the events of Akbar's reign but also celebrate the intellectual and artistic achievements of his time.

Administration and Governance: The Mughal Model

Centralized Authority and Bureaucratic Excellence

The administrative apparatus of the Mughal Empire was one of its most significant legacies. The Mughals established a highly centralized system that combined military power with a sophisticated bureaucracy. This system was designed to manage a vast and diverse empire, ensuring that even remote regions were integrated into the central governance framework.

The Mughal bureaucracy was staffed by officials selected on the basis of merit, with positions often filled by talented individuals from various religious and ethnic backgrounds. The introduction of the mansabdari system—a hierarchical system of ranks that determined an officer's salary, military responsibilities, and administrative duties—ensured a degree of standardization and accountability. In *Mughal Administration*, historian V.D. Mahajan explains how the mansabdari system was instrumental in maintaining control over the empire's expansive territories while also fostering loyalty among the officers.

Revenue collection under the Mughals was both efficient and innovative. Land revenue, which formed the backbone of the empire's income, was assessed using detailed surveys and standardized measurements. This system not only maximized the state's revenue but also provided a measure of fairness in taxation, helping to sustain the empire's economic stability.

Works like *The Mughal Economy* by Andre Wink delve into the intricacies of this system, highlighting how the Mughals balanced fiscal responsibility with the need to support a vast and diverse populace.

Judicial and Legal Reforms

Mughal governance was also characterized by significant judicial and legal reforms. The empire developed a comprehensive legal framework that drew from Islamic law (Sharia) while accommodating local customs and traditions. This dual legal system allowed for a flexible approach to governance, wherein different communities could adhere to their traditional practices under the overarching authority of the Mughal court.

Emperor Akbar, in particular, was known for his progressive legal reforms. His policy of Sulh-i-Kul (universal tolerance) extended beyond religious matters to include judicial practices, ensuring that justice was administered impartially. In his efforts to reform the legal system, Akbar sought the counsel of scholars and jurists from various backgrounds, thereby creating a more inclusive and effective framework. These reforms are detailed in texts such as *Akbar: The Great Mughal* by Ira Mukhoty, which examines how Akbar's legal innovations contributed to the empire's long-term stability and prosperity.

Economic and Social Policies

The Mughal rulers also implemented policies that promoted economic growth and social welfare. Agricultural reforms, improvements in irrigation, and the development of road networks all contributed to a flourishing economy. The establishment of trade relations, both within the empire and with external markets, helped integrate India into a global economic system. Markets buzzed with activity, and urban centers became hubs of commerce, art, and culture.

Mughal patronage extended to social and cultural institutions as well. The emperors commissioned the construction of public works, such as gardens, fountains, and caravanserais, which enhanced the quality of life for their subjects. These projects not only beautified the cities but also served practical purposes, such as providing rest stops for travelers and boosting local economies. Historians like John F. Richards, in *The Mughal Empire*, argue that such initiatives were crucial in forging a sense of shared identity and community among the diverse populations of the empire.

Cultural Syncretism and the Lasting Legacy of the Mughals

The Blend of Diverse Traditions

The Mughal legacy is best understood as a dynamic fusion of diverse cultural influences. The empire's rulers were patrons of a multicultural court that brought together Persian elegance, Central Asian vigor, and the rich, indigenous traditions of India. This confluence of influences resulted in a cultural milieu that was both refined and robust—a synthesis that enriched every aspect of Mughal life, from art and literature to music and cuisine.

The literary and artistic productions of the Mughal era exemplify this cultural blend. Persian, as the court language, provided a common medium through which artists and intellectuals could communicate their ideas. At the same time, local languages and traditions infused Mughal culture with a distinctive Indian character. This fusion is eloquently explored in works such as *The Mughal World: India's Tainted Paradise* by Abraham Eraly, which examines how the interplay of different traditions created a legacy of artistic and cultural innovation that continues to resonate today.

Enduring Influences on Modern India

The impact of the Mughal period on modern India is profound and multifaceted. The architectural landmarks built by the Mughals continue to attract global admiration and serve as symbols of India's historical grandeur. The administrative innovations and policies of inclusion established during this era laid the groundwork for later forms of governance and legal systems in the subcontinent. Moreover, the Mughal emphasis on cultural syncretism remains a defining feature of India's pluralistic society.

Contemporary scholars frequently draw parallels between Mughal policies of tolerance and the ideals of modern secular democracy. For instance, in *In Search of the Mughal World*, historian Annemarie Schimmel underscores how the Mughals' patronage of diverse cultural traditions paved the way for a society that values pluralism and inclusivity. This legacy is evident in India's ongoing celebration of festivals, culinary traditions, and art forms that bear the unmistakable imprint of Mughal influence.

Reflections on a Timeless Legacy

In reflecting on the Mughal legacy, it is important to recognize that the empire was not without its challenges and contradictions. Like any great civilization, the Mughals grappled with issues of succession, religious tensions, and the complexities of administering a vast, heterogeneous empire. Yet, the lasting impact of their achievements—whether in the form of breathtaking monuments, innovative administrative systems, or the rich cultural tapestry they wove—testifies to their enduring influence on Indian history.

As we examine the Mughal period, we see a narrative of both triumph and transformation—a story of how an empire can rise from the confluence of diverse traditions to create a legacy that transcends time and borders. The Mughal experience serves as a reminder of the transformative power of art, the importance of inclusive governance, and the potential for cultural synthesis to create something greater than the sum of its parts.

Concluding Thoughts

The Mughal legacy remains one of the most celebrated and influential chapters in the history of India. Through visionary leadership, artistic brilliance, and administrative innovation, the Mughals forged an empire that was as rich in cultural diversity as it was in political power. Their contributions—visible in the majestic monuments, the intricate miniatures, and the sophisticated bureaucracy—continue to inspire and inform our understanding of Indian civilization.

For readers seeking to delve deeper into the Mughal era, works such as Abraham Eraly's *The Mughal Throne: The Saga of India's*

Great Emperors, Ira Mukhoty's *Akbar: The Great Mughal*, and Catherine Asher's *Mughal Architecture: An Outline of Its History and Development* provide invaluable insights into the myriad dimensions of Mughal rule. These texts, along with many others, highlight the complexity and beauty of a period that not only defined a nation's past but also continues to shape its present and future.

As we conclude this exploration of the Mughal legacy, it is clear that their influence extends far beyond the realm of art and architecture. The Mughals set into motion processes of cultural integration and administrative reform that have left a lasting imprint on the subcontinent. Their story is one of ambition, creativity, and resilience—a story that continues to echo in the modern landscapes of India, inviting us to reflect on the enduring power of human ingenuity and the transformative potential of cultural synthesis.

In celebrating the achievements of the Mughals, we honor a tradition that, despite its complexities, remains a testament to the possibility of building bridges across cultural divides. It is a legacy that reminds us that true greatness is often found at the intersection of diverse traditions—a place where art meets administration, where military power is tempered by wisdom, and where the dreams of a bygone era continue to inspire the modern world.

6

Colonial Confluences – European Arrival and the British Raj

The arrival of European powers in India marked a watershed moment in the subcontinent's long and complex history. This chapter delves into the transformative era of colonialism—from early maritime encounters and trading posts to the gradual imposition of British colonial rule. The interplay of indigenous resilience and foreign dominance created a unique socio-political landscape, the reverberations of which are still evident today. Drawing on scholarly works such as John Keay's *India: A History*, Jawaharlal Nehru's *The Discovery of India*, and Shashi Tharoor's *Inglorious Empire*, we explore how colonialism reshaped India's economy, society, and political identity.

The Dawn of European Contact

Early Maritime Encounters and Trade

The first significant European contact with India began in the late 15th century, when Portuguese explorers, led by Vasco da Gama, sailed around the Cape of Good Hope to reach the shores of Calicut in 1498. This breakthrough opened new sea routes that transformed global trade networks. The Portuguese established a string of coastal enclaves, forging an initial path for European influence in the Indian Ocean.

These early interactions were primarily driven by commerce. European powers sought to control the spice trade, which had long been a lucrative enterprise for Indian, Arab, and Persian merchants. The establishment of trading posts along the Malabar Coast, and later at strategic locations such as Goa, marked the beginning of sustained European engagement in Indian economic affairs. John Keay, in *India: A History*, details how these trading ventures laid the foundation for future imperial ambitions by integrating India into an emerging global economy.

Competition Among European Powers

Following the Portuguese, other European nations—including the Dutch, French, and British—entered the fray. The Dutch established the Dutch East India Company (VOC), and the French set up their own trading enterprises, creating a competitive environment that increasingly centered on control over trade routes and regional markets. By the early 17th century, India had become a focal point for European rivalry, with each nation seeking to secure economic advantages.

This period of competition catalyzed technological and navigational innovations. European naval advancements, coupled with a better understanding of monsoon winds and local maritime routes, allowed these powers to penetrate deeper into the Indian subcontinent. Works like *The Portuguese in India* by K. M. Mathew provide detailed accounts of the early interactions and highlight the complex web of trade, diplomacy, and conflict that characterized this era.

The Rise of the British East India Company

Establishment and Expansion of Trade Networks

Among the European contenders, the British East India Company emerged as the most influential. Established in 1600, the Company initially focused on trade, importing spices, textiles, and other commodities. Over time, its influence grew as it established trading posts in major port cities such as Surat, Bombay (now Mumbai), and Calcutta (now Kolkata). The Company's ability to negotiate favorable terms with local rulers and exploit rivalries among regional powers allowed it to expand its reach across the subcontinent.

The transition from a trading entity to a territorial power was gradual. The British East India Company skillfully leveraged economic might to secure political concessions, forging alliances and even engaging in military conflicts when necessary. As Shashi Tharoor discusses in *Inglorious Empire*, the Company's dual role as both merchant and conqueror set the stage for the eventual establishment of direct British colonial rule over India.

Administrative Innovations and Military Prowess

The British East India Company introduced a range of administrative innovations that profoundly altered the governance of India. Its system of revenue collection, most notably the Permanent Settlement of 1793 implemented in Bengal, restructured the agrarian economy and reshaped the relationship between the state and rural populations. This policy, as explained by John Keay, was designed to create a class of loyal landlords who would act as intermediaries between the colonial administration and the peasantry, ensuring a steady flow of revenue to finance British interests.

Simultaneously, the Company built a formidable military force. Its private armies, composed of both European officers and locally recruited sepoys, played a critical role in expanding and consolidating British control. The Battle of Plassey in 1757, a decisive victory against the Nawab of Bengal, is often cited as the turning point that signaled the rise of British dominance in India. This military conquest not only dismantled regional power structures but also provided the Company with the resources to further entrench its administrative and economic systems.

The British Raj: Transition from Company to Crown

The End of Company Rule

By the mid-19th century, the cumulative effects of Company rule had generated widespread discontent among Indians. Issues such as high taxation, exploitative revenue practices, and cultural insensitivity fueled a growing sense of injustice. The Indian Rebellion of 1857, also known as the Sepoy Mutiny, was a dramatic, albeit ultimately unsuccessful, expression of this discontent. While the uprising was suppressed, it served as a catalyst for a significant shift in colonial policy.

In the aftermath of the rebellion, the British government decided to take direct control of India. The Government of India Act of 1858 formally transferred authority from the East India Company to the British Crown, ushering in the period known as the British Raj. Jawaharlal Nehru's *The Discovery of India* reflects on this transition as a moment of profound transformation—one in which the mechanisms of colonial exploitation were restructured, yet many of the underlying policies remained intact.

Governance, Reforms, and the Modern State

Under the British Raj, India was administered through a complex system that combined direct rule by British officials with the retention of certain traditional structures. The colonial administration introduced reforms aimed at modernizing the economy, legal systems, and infrastructure. Railways, telegraphs, and modern banking systems were established, transforming the economic landscape and knitting together the diverse regions of the subcontinent.

However, these reforms were double-edged. While they facilitated economic development and modernization, they also served to entrench British control and extract wealth from India. Historians such as Shashi Tharoor argue in *Inglorious Empire* that the benefits of British modernization were largely outweighed by the costs of exploitation, leading to long-term economic and social disparities that continue to influence India today.

The British legal system, for instance, was introduced with the intention of creating a uniform code of law. Yet, it also undermined indigenous legal traditions and altered the fabric of local societies. Similarly, while the construction of railways boosted commerce and mobility, it also facilitated the rapid movement of colonial troops and resources, further consolidating British power. These contradictions underscore the complex legacy of British colonialism—a legacy that, despite its achievements in infrastructure and administration, was marred by economic extraction and cultural disruption.

Social and Cultural Impacts

Educational and Intellectual Transformations

One of the most lasting legacies of British colonialism was the transformation of the Indian educational system. The introduction of Western-style education, with English as the medium of instruction, created a new class of Indians who were conversant with modern scientific and political ideas. This class, often referred to as the "brown intelligentsia," played a pivotal role in the eventual struggle for independence. Figures such as Raja Ram Mohan Roy and later Mahatma Gandhi were deeply influenced by Western liberal thought and the principles of democracy and human rights.

The educational reforms introduced by the British were documented in works like *The Great Partition: The Making of India and Pakistan* by Yasmin Khan, which details how modern education contributed to the rise of nationalist sentiment and political awareness. While these reforms were instrumental in creating a modern bureaucratic and intellectual elite, they also marked a departure from traditional Indian systems of learning, leading to a complex interplay between old and new forms of knowledge.

Cultural Exchanges and the Emergence of a Hybrid Identity

British rule also engendered significant cultural exchanges. Indian society absorbed elements of British culture, such as legal practices, administrative methods, and educational ideals, while also influencing British perceptions of India. This reciprocal exchange resulted in a hybrid cultural identity that persists in various forms today. The legacy of colonial art, literature, and even cuisine is visible in modern India—a fusion that reflects centuries of cross-cultural interaction.

In *The Discovery of India*, Jawaharlal Nehru reflects on how the colonial encounter, despite its many injustices, also catalyzed intellectual and cultural ferment. The colonial period saw the rise of Indian literature in English and the emergence of new artistic styles that blended traditional Indian motifs with European techniques. This synthesis of cultural forms became a cornerstone of modern Indian identity, providing a framework for both resistance to and reinterpretation of colonial legacies.

Resistance, Reform, and the Quest for Independence

The social and cultural upheavals triggered by British colonial policies eventually led to a burgeoning independence movement. Intellectuals, reformers, and revolutionaries from diverse backgrounds united in their quest to reclaim India's sovereignty. The struggle for independence was characterized by both violent uprisings and non-violent protests, reflecting the multifaceted nature of colonial resistance.

Leaders such as Mahatma Gandhi and Jawaharlal Nehru emerged as central figures in this movement. Their philosophies, which blended traditional Indian values with modern ideas of civil rights and democracy, resonated with millions of Indians. The Indian National Congress, established in 1885, became the primary platform for articulating nationalist aspirations and mobilizing support against colonial rule. The evolution of these movements is extensively chronicled in works like *India After Gandhi* by Ramachandra Guha, which provides a comprehensive account of the post-independence challenges that stemmed from the colonial experience.

Reflections on the Colonial Legacy

Economic Exploitation and Structural Changes

The economic legacy of British colonialism remains one of its most contentious aspects. The extraction of wealth through heavy taxation, the imposition of cash crop economies, and the systematic deindustrialization of traditional sectors led to significant economic challenges that India has grappled with long after independence. Historians like Shashi Tharoor in *Inglorious Empire* highlight how colonial economic policies not only enriched the British Empire but also left India with structural imbalances that hindered its post-colonial development.

Despite these challenges, the infrastructural developments initiated during the colonial period—such as railways, telegraphs, and modern administrative institutions—played a crucial role in integrating India into the global economy. This dual legacy of exploitation and modernization continues to influence India's economic trajectory, prompting ongoing debates about the true costs and benefits of colonial rule.

The Cultural and Political Renaissance

Beyond its economic dimensions, British colonialism also precipitated a cultural and political renaissance in India. The exposure to modern ideas of governance, science, and human rights laid the intellectual groundwork for a renewed vision of Indian society—one that sought to reconcile its rich historical traditions with the imperatives of modernity. The resulting political discourse was characterized by debates about identity, progress, and self-determination that continue to shape India's democratic ethos today.

In reflecting on this transformative era, Jawaharlal Nehru's *The Discovery of India* provides a nuanced perspective on how colonial rule, despite its many adversities, contributed to the emergence of a modern, secular, and pluralistic nation-state. Nehru argued that the process of colonial domination, with all its contradictions, ultimately catalyzed a reawakening of Indian self-consciousness—a reawakening that led to the vibrant struggle for independence and the eventual formation of a sovereign republic.

Concluding Thoughts

The era of colonial confluences and the British Raj represents one of the most complex and transformative chapters in Indian history. From the initial encounters with European traders to the eventual subjugation and reorganization of Indian society under British rule, this period was marked by profound shifts in economic, social, and political paradigms. The legacy of colonialism is a double-edged sword: while it introduced modern administrative and infrastructural systems that continue to underpin India's development, it also inflicted deep economic and cultural wounds that India has been striving to heal for over a century.

For those seeking a deeper understanding of this transformative period, works such as John Keay's *India: A History*, Jawaharlal Nehru's *The Discovery of India*, and Shashi Tharoor's *Inglorious Empire* offer rich, critical insights into the ways colonialism redefined the Indian landscape. These texts underscore the multifaceted nature of British rule—its achievements, its excesses, and its enduring impact on the nation's collective psyche.

In examining the colonial era, we are reminded that history is a dialogue between multiple forces and voices. The British Raj was not a monolithic imposition but a dynamic interplay of power, resistance, innovation, and adaptation. The legacies of this period continue to inform debates about national identity, economic policy, and cultural heritage in contemporary India. As we move forward in our exploration of Indian history, the lessons of colonial confluences prompt us to consider how the intersections of tradition and modernity can shape a nation's destiny.

The story of colonial India is, ultimately, a story of transformation—a process in which external influences were both resisted and assimilated, creating a new cultural and political landscape that paved the way for modern India. It is a narrative that challenges us to grapple with the complexities of power, progress, and identity, and one that remains as relevant today as it was in the tumultuous centuries of colonial rule.

In summary, the colonial period set in motion a series of

profound changes that reshaped every facet of Indian life. It was an era of contrasts: of exploitation and modernization, of cultural imposition and intellectual renaissance, of economic hardship and infrastructural progress. These complexities are integral to understanding the historical forces that eventually led to India's emergence as an independent nation—a nation that continues to negotiate the legacies of its colonial past while charting a course toward the future.

7

The Freedom Struggle – Seeds of Nationalism and Revolution

The story of India's freedom struggle is a tapestry woven with the threads of sacrifice, perseverance, and a visionary quest for self-determination. This chapter traces the evolution of Indian nationalism from its early stirrings to a full-blown mass movement that ultimately led to independence. Drawing on seminal works such as Jawaharlal Nehru's *The Discovery of India*, Bipan Chandra's *India's Struggle for Independence*, and *Freedom at Midnight* by Larry Collins and Dominique Lapierre, we examine how ideas of freedom and justice ignited passions across a vast and diverse nation, uniting millions under the banner of a common cause.

Early Incubation of National Consciousness

The Impact of Colonial Policies

British colonial policies, with their systematic exploitation and cultural arrogance, laid the groundwork for dissent. Over decades, the economic hardships imposed by heavy taxation and the deindustrialization of traditional sectors began to erode the social fabric of Indian society. These measures, while intended to maximize colonial profit, inadvertently sowed the seeds of discontent among various strata of the population. Indian intellectuals, reformers, and common people alike began questioning the legitimacy of foreign rule.

In *The Discovery of India*, Jawaharlal Nehru reflects on how centuries of exploitative policies under the British not only stripped India of its wealth but also undermined its cultural and moral foundations. This disenchantment with colonial governance catalyzed a search for indigenous ideas of self-governance and cultural renaissance. The early reform movements led by figures such as Raja Ram Mohan Roy and Ishwar Chandra Vidyasagar introduced modern educational reforms, social activism, and critiques of traditional hierarchies, thereby creating a climate in which the idea of freedom could take root.

Intellectual Awakening and the Role of Print Media

The 19th century witnessed a remarkable intellectual awakening, aided by the advent of print media and an emerging educated middle class. Newspapers, journals, and pamphlets became the vehicles for the dissemination of nationalist ideas. These publications not only informed the public about the injustices of colonial rule but also provided a forum for debating new political philosophies. Editors and writers such as Bal

Gangadhar Tilak and Bipin Chandra Pal became the voices of a growing public that yearned for change.

Works like Bipan Chandra's *India's Struggle for Independence* underscore how these early efforts of journalism and literary expression contributed to a broader cultural and political awakening. The written word became a rallying point for the masses, nurturing a sense of shared identity and destiny that transcended regional, linguistic, and religious differences.

Emergence of Organized Nationalism

The Formation of the Indian National Congress

One of the pivotal milestones in the freedom struggle was the formation of the Indian National Congress (INC) in 1885. Founded by a small group of educated elites, the Congress initially functioned as a forum for airing grievances and seeking moderate reforms. Its early leaders, such as Dadabhai Naoroji and Gopal Krishna Gokhale, believed in gradual political change through dialogue and constitutional means. They worked to expose the economic drain imposed by colonial policies and to argue for greater Indian participation in governance.

Over time, the INC evolved from a body of moderate reformers into a dynamic platform for radical ideas. As the movement progressed, internal debates emerged over the pace and nature of change, setting the stage for a larger, more inclusive struggle that would ultimately encompass all segments of society. Nehru's *The Discovery of India* provides insights into these formative years, highlighting how the initial moderate stance eventually gave way to more assertive demands for complete independence.

Revolutionary Movements and the Fight from the Margins

While the Congress sought change through constitutional means, a parallel stream of revolutionary activity was also gathering momentum. Inspired by global movements for liberation and emboldened by their own cultural pride, groups of young radicals began to advocate for direct action against British rule. These revolutionaries, influenced by both Gandhian ideas and Marxist thought, engaged in acts of sabotage, armed resistance, and clandestine operations against colonial institutions.

Figures such as Bhagat Singh, Chandrashekhar Azad, and Subhas Chandra Bose became iconic symbols of this militant resistance. Their actions, as documented in various biographies and historical studies, underscored a deep-seated belief that true freedom could only be achieved through complete overthrow of the oppressive system. *Freedom at Midnight* vividly recounts episodes of armed struggle and daring escapes, emphasizing the risks these revolutionaries took to disrupt colonial authority. Their efforts, though often met with brutal repression, energized a generation of Indians who refused to be subjugated.

The Gandhian Era: Nonviolence as a Weapon

Mahatma Gandhi's Philosophy and Leadership

Mahatma Gandhi emerged as the preeminent leader of the freedom struggle by championing a philosophy that combined moral clarity with pragmatic resistance. Influenced by his experiences in South Africa and his deep commitment to Indian spiritual traditions, Gandhi developed the principles of Satyagraha (truth-force) and nonviolent civil disobedience. His methods offered a stark contrast to the violent confrontations of the earlier revolutionary movements, emphasizing instead the power of peaceful protest to challenge injustice.

Gandhi's leadership transformed the INC and the broader nationalist movement. His ability to mobilize millions, from peasants in rural villages to urban workers, was unprecedented. Through campaigns such as the Non-Cooperation Movement (1920–22), the Salt March (1930), and the Quit India Movement (1942), Gandhi demonstrated that nonviolence could be a potent tool against an empire built on the use of force. His ideas and actions are extensively detailed in Jawaharlal Nehru's *The Discovery of India*, which portrays Gandhi not only as a political leader but also as a moral guide whose vision transcended the immediate struggles of his time.

Mass Mobilization and Civil Disobedience

Gandhi's nonviolent strategies sparked widespread participation in the freedom movement. Ordinary Indians—farmers, laborers, students, and women—joined the struggle, transforming it from a debate among elites into a mass movement that spanned the entire nation. Public protests, boycotts of British goods, and refusal to pay taxes became everyday acts of resistance. These actions challenged the very legitimacy of colonial rule by demonstrating that the power of the people could not be easily suppressed.

The mobilization of the masses also led to the development of new forms of political organization. Grassroots committees and local councils sprang up across India, serving as the backbone of the movement and facilitating communication between distant regions. This decentralized network of resistance became a formidable counterforce to the centralized machinery of British governance, as detailed by Bipan Chandra in *India's Struggle for Independence*. The collaborative spirit that emerged during this period forged a national identity rooted in the shared aspirations for justice and self-governance.

The Road to Independence

Negotiations, Crises, and Concessions

By the 1940s, the cumulative pressure of decades of struggle had forced the British government to reexamine its hold on India. A series of negotiations and constitutional reforms were introduced in an attempt to placate growing nationalist demands. However, these concessions were often seen by Indian leaders as half-measures that failed to address the fundamental inequities of colonial rule.

The turmoil of World War II further strained British resources and resolve. The war exacerbated economic hardships in India and intensified demands for immediate self-rule. During this critical period, leaders like Mahatma Gandhi, Jawaharlal Nehru, and Sardar Patel argued that independence was not only desirable but inevitable. Their debates and discussions, recorded in various archival documents and chronicled in *Freedom at Midnight*, reveal the intense political negotiations that characterized the final years of colonial rule.

Partition and the Birth of Modern Nations

The culmination of the freedom struggle came in 1947 with the decision to partition British India into two separate nations: India and Pakistan. This momentous event was the result of complex political negotiations, religious divisions, and the urgency to end colonial domination. While the partition marked the achievement of independence for millions, it also unleashed communal violence and mass migrations that left deep scars on the subcontinent.

The pain of partition, with its massive human displacement and tragic loss of life, has been the subject of numerous scholarly works. Historian Ramachandra Guha, in *India After Gandhi*, discusses how the process of partition, despite its harrowing consequences, set the stage for the emergence of modern democratic institutions in India. The bitter legacy of partition continues to influence political and social discourse in the region, serving as a reminder of the complexities involved in forging national identities.

Reflections on the Freedom Struggle

The Triumph of Collective Action

The freedom struggle was, at its core, a triumph of collective action over oppressive structures. The movement was not driven by a single leader or ideology but was the result of the cumulative efforts of millions of Indians from diverse backgrounds. The shared commitment to justice, equality, and self-determination united disparate communities in a common cause—a unity that persists as a defining feature of modern

India.

The narrative of India's struggle for independence is enriched by the diverse contributions of its leaders and participants. Whether it was the philosophical insights of Gandhi, the strategic acumen of Nehru, the revolutionary zeal of Bhagat Singh, or the grassroots mobilization by countless unnamed citizens, each played a role in shaping a movement that was both inclusive and transformative. The multifaceted nature of the struggle, as elaborated in Bipan Chandra's works, underscores the power of unity in the face of systemic injustice.

Legacy and Lessons for the Future

The legacy of the freedom struggle extends far beyond the attainment of independence. The ideals and methods that underpinned the movement continue to inspire contemporary struggles for justice and human rights around the world. The emphasis on nonviolence, democratic participation, and social equality remains a potent force in modern political discourse, not only in India but globally.

Reflecting on the freedom struggle, one cannot help but acknowledge the profound impact it has had on shaping India's national identity. The movement catalyzed a cultural and political renaissance that redefined what it meant to be Indian— a people united by a shared vision of progress, diversity, and democratic governance. Works like *The Discovery of India* serve as enduring testaments to the transformative power of a movement driven by the collective will of a nation.

Concluding Thoughts

The struggle for independence was a defining chapter in India's history—one marked by immense sacrifice, visionary leadership, and the unyielding spirit of a nation determined to reclaim its destiny. From early intellectual awakenings and moderate reform efforts to revolutionary actions and mass mobilizations, the freedom struggle was an evolving process that encapsulated the aspirations and dreams of millions. It was a battle fought on multiple fronts: economic, cultural, political, and moral.

In examining this tumultuous period, the insights provided by Jawaharlal Nehru in *The Discovery of India*, Bipan Chandra's detailed analysis in *India's Struggle for Independence*, and the dramatic narrative of *Freedom at Midnight* collectively offer a comprehensive understanding of how India emerged from centuries of colonial subjugation to become a sovereign nation.

Today, as modern India grapples with the challenges and opportunities of a globalized world, the lessons of the freedom struggle remain as relevant as ever. They remind us that the quest for justice and self-determination is an ongoing process—one that requires vigilance, unity, and a steadfast commitment to the ideals of liberty and equality.

The legacy of the freedom struggle is not merely confined to historical memory; it lives on in the democratic institutions, cultural expressions, and the vibrant civic life of contemporary India. As we reflect on this pivotal era, we honor the sacrifices of those who fought for independence and acknowledge that their struggle was, and continues to be, a source of inspiration for generations striving to build a just and inclusive society.

In closing, the freedom struggle stands as a powerful testament to the capacity of collective action to overcome even the most entrenched systems of oppression. It is a reminder that the pursuit of freedom, however arduous, is a noble endeavor that transforms not only nations but the very spirit of humanity.

8

Partition and New Beginnings – The Birth of Modern Nations

Few events in modern Indian history have been as transformative—and as painful—as the partition of 1947. In this chapter, we explore the processes, controversies, and consequences of partition, as well as the subsequent efforts to build two independent nations from the ruins of a colonial past. Drawing on seminal works such as Ramachandra Guha's *India After Gandhi*, Khushwant Singh's *A History of the Punjab*, and Yasmin Khan's *The Great Partition: The Making of India and Pakistan*, we examine how partition reshaped identities, redrew borders, and laid the foundations for modern nationhood in South Asia.

The Road to Partition

Historical Context and Political Negotiations

The seeds of partition were sown long before 1947. The British colonial strategy of "divide and rule," which emphasized communal differences between Hindus and Muslims, had steadily undermined the prospects for a unified national movement. During the decades of British rule, political leaders from diverse communities voiced their concerns over representation, economic rights, and cultural autonomy. As the struggle for independence intensified, these long-standing divisions came to the forefront.

Political negotiations in the 1940s reflected this deep-seated discord. The Cabinet Mission Plan of 1946, for example, attempted to preserve a united India while granting extensive provincial autonomy. However, mounting distrust between the Indian National Congress and the Muslim League, led by Muhammad Ali Jinnah, ultimately rendered such solutions unworkable. In *The Great Partition: The Making of India and Pakistan*, Yasmin Khan details how successive proposals for power-sharing collapsed amid fears of majoritarian rule and the specter of communal violence.

The Moment of Decision

By mid-1947, it became increasingly clear to both British administrators and Indian political leaders that a united independent India was no longer a viable option. The announcement of British withdrawal precipitated a hurried series of negotiations, leading to the decision to partition the subcontinent into two separate nations—India and Pakistan. This decision, formalized through the Mountbatten Plan, was driven by the desire to quell communal strife but was also marred by an inherent lack of consensus and preparation.

The hurried nature of the partition process is vividly recounted in Khushwant Singh's *A History of the Punjab*. Singh notes that the rapid redrawing of borders, often along arbitrary lines, sowed the seeds for future conflict. The boundary demarcation, led by the Radcliffe Commission, was completed in just a few weeks—an astonishingly short period for a process that would alter the lives of millions. This abruptness, as many historians argue, contributed to the mass dislocation and communal violence that ensued.

The Human Cost of Partition

Mass Migrations and Communal Violence

The immediate aftermath of partition was characterized by one of the largest mass migrations in human history. Hindus and Sikhs in what was to become Pakistan, and Muslims in India, found themselves on the "wrong" side of the new borders. Trains, buses, and makeshift vehicles became vessels for millions fleeing violence, uncertainty, and a complete upheaval of their lives. Accounts of these migrations, as documented in *Freedom at Midnight* by Larry Collins and Dominique Lapierre, paint a harrowing picture of chaos, loss, and enduring trauma.

Communal violence erupted on an unprecedented scale. Entire towns were razed, and lives were lost in violent clashes between communities that had, until then, coexisted for centuries. Eyewitness testimonies and archival reports reveal a pattern of brutality that defies simple explanation—a human tragedy marked by betrayal, fear, and the collapse of social order. Historians like Ramachandra Guha, in *India After Gandhi*, stress that the communal discord unleashed during partition not only claimed hundreds of thousands of lives but also left deep psychological scars on survivors, fundamentally altering the collective memory of the subcontinent.

The Social and Psychological Impact

The legacy of partition is felt not only in the physical relocation of populations but also in the deep divisions it sowed in the social fabric. Families were torn apart, communities fractured, and long-standing cultural ties were abruptly severed. The forced displacement resulted in the loss of ancestral homes, livelihoods, and cultural heritage for millions, while the ensuing violence instilled a lingering sense of mistrust and alienation among communities.

In his extensive analysis, Guha emphasizes that the trauma of partition has shaped the identities of both India and Pakistan, creating a historical wound that continues to influence their political and social landscapes. The struggle to come to terms with this past has been reflected in literature, art, and public discourse, as each generation attempts to reconcile with the legacy of division and loss.

Building New Nations: The Challenges of Statecraft

Establishing Political Institutions

Despite the chaos and grief, the post-partition period also witnessed the emergence of new political frameworks and institutions designed to govern diverse and often divided populations. India, inheriting a rich legacy of democratic traditions and a robust constitutional framework, embarked on the arduous task of nation-building. The drafting of the Indian Constitution, a monumental effort led by figures such as Dr. B.R. Ambedkar, sought to create a secular, inclusive, and democratic state that would respect the rights and aspirations of its diverse citizens.

In *The Discovery of India*, Jawaharlal Nehru reflects on the challenges of creating a new political order from the ruins of colonialism and communal strife. The Indian Constitution was conceived as a document that balanced individual rights with social justice, and it enshrined principles of equality, freedom, and fraternity. The process of constitution-making, as described by scholars such as Granville Austin in *The Indian Constitution: Cornerstone of a Nation*, was a remarkable exercise in consensus-building, drawing on the experiences and sacrifices of the freedom struggle.

Economic Reconstruction and Social Welfare

Both India and Pakistan faced immense challenges in reconstructing their shattered economies. Partition had disrupted traditional economic networks, severed critical transportation and communication links, and resulted in the displacement of millions of skilled workers and entrepreneurs. The task of economic reconstruction involved not only rebuilding infrastructure but also reimagining economic policies to foster development and stability.

In India, economic planning became a central feature of post-independence governance. The establishment of institutions like the Planning Commission aimed to channel resources toward industrialization, agricultural reform, and social welfare programs. Historians such as Amartya Sen have noted that the early economic policies of independent India were deeply influenced by the desire to overcome the structural imbalances left by colonial exploitation and the disruptive legacy of partition.

Pakistan, on the other hand, had to navigate the challenges of building a new state with limited resources and a predominantly agrarian economy. The newly formed nation embarked on its own journey of nation-building, which included efforts to modernize its economic infrastructure, address regional disparities, and forge a national identity amidst ongoing communal tensions. Works like *Pakistan: A Hard Country* by Anatol Lieven provide a detailed account of how Pakistan grappled with the dual challenges of economic development and political consolidation in the early years of independence.

Social Integration and Cultural Renaissance

In the wake of partition, both India and Pakistan confronted the monumental task of fostering social integration and healing the wounds of communal strife. In India, the ethos of secularism and pluralism was enshrined in both the Constitution and the broader national narrative. Efforts were made to integrate refugees and displaced communities into the social and economic fabric of the nation. Programs aimed at resettlement, education, and social welfare were launched to help those affected by the violence of partition rebuild their lives.

At the same time, the post-partition period witnessed a cultural renaissance that sought to reinterpret the legacy of division in creative and constructive ways. Indian literature, cinema, and art began to explore themes of identity, loss, and resilience, offering both catharsis and a vision for a more inclusive future. In *India After Gandhi*, Ramachandra Guha documents how the creative arts became a powerful medium for addressing the traumas of partition and celebrating the newfound diversity of modern India.

In Pakistan, the process of forging a national identity was similarly complex. The creation of a state based on Islamic principles was intended to provide a unifying cultural framework, yet the diversity of its population—comprising various ethnicities, languages, and traditions—posed significant challenges. Intellectuals and political leaders in Pakistan worked to articulate a vision of national identity that could reconcile these differences and create a sense of common purpose. The evolution of Pakistani identity, as explored in works such as *The Idea of Pakistan* by Stephen Philip Cohen, remains an ongoing dialogue between tradition and modernity.

Legacy and Long-Term Implications

The Political and Geopolitical Landscape

The partition of India and the subsequent creation of Pakistan fundamentally altered the geopolitical landscape of South Asia. The borders drawn in 1947 have been the source of enduring conflict, most notably over the disputed region of Kashmir, which continues to fuel tensions between the two nations. The legacy of partition is thus inseparable from the broader challenges of regional stability and international relations in South Asia.

The political institutions established in the wake of partition have also had lasting implications. In India, the democratic experiment has endured as a testament to the resilience and adaptability of its constitutional framework, despite numerous challenges. In Pakistan, the interplay between democratic and military rule has shaped the nation's political trajectory, influencing everything from governance to civil-military relations. The enduring legacies of partition, as analyzed in *India After Gandhi* and other scholarly works, continue to inform debates about national identity, sovereignty, and regional cooperation.

Collective Memory and the Search for Reconciliation

Partition remains one of the most significant and painful episodes in the collective memory of both India and Pakistan. Its impact is evident in the literature, art, and public discourse of both nations, where themes of loss, displacement, and the search for reconciliation are ever-present. The process of coming to terms with partition is ongoing, as each generation seeks to understand and heal the wounds of the past.

Public commemorations, memorials, and educational initiatives have all played a role in shaping the narrative of partition. These efforts, while often controversial, reflect a broader societal recognition of the need to confront historical injustices in order to build a more inclusive future. Scholars like Guha and Khan have argued that acknowledging the full complexity of partition is essential for overcoming the lingering divisions that continue to influence inter-community relations in South Asia.

Concluding Reflections: New Beginnings Amid Old Wounds

The partition of 1947 was both an end and a beginning—a moment of profound loss that gave way to the birth of new nations and the promise of self-determination. In the wake of partition, India and Pakistan embarked on parallel journeys of nation-building, each grappling with the dual imperatives of healing past wounds and forging a future rooted in their respective visions of identity and progress.

For India, the post-partition era marked the beginning of a

democratic experiment that sought to integrate vast cultural, linguistic, and religious diversities under a single constitutional framework. The process of rebuilding, despite immense challenges, was underpinned by a commitment to secularism, social justice, and economic development. As *India After Gandhi* attests, the challenges of partition became catalysts for transformative reforms and a renewed vision of what modern India could become.

For Pakistan, the challenges were equally formidable. The task of unifying a disparate population under the banner of an Islamic state required both political ingenuity and a willingness to embrace complexity. The early years of Pakistan were marked by intense debates about identity, governance, and the role of religion in public life—a legacy that continues to shape Pakistani society today, as explored in *Pakistan: A Hard Country* and *The Idea of Pakistan*.

Ultimately, the legacy of partition is a testament to the resilience of the human spirit in the face of overwhelming adversity. It is a legacy that reminds us that even amid profound tragedy, new beginnings are possible. The stories of countless individuals who survived displacement, violence, and loss are woven into the fabric of modern South Asia, offering enduring lessons about the cost of division and the possibility of reconciliation.

As we reflect on this pivotal chapter in Indian and Pakistani history, we are reminded that the journey toward nationhood is an ongoing process—one that requires continual engagement with the past in order to build a more just, inclusive, and peaceful future. The legacy of partition challenges us to confront our shared histories with honesty and compassion, and to honor the sacrifices of those who endured its hardships.

For further insights into this transformative period, readers may consult Yasmin Khan's *The Great Partition: The Making of India and Pakistan*, Ramachandra Guha's *India After Gandhi*, and Khushwant Singh's *A History of the Punjab*. These works offer complementary perspectives that deepen our understanding of how partition not only redrew borders but also reshaped the identities and destinies of entire nations.

In conclusion, the partition of 1947 remains one of the most defining moments in the modern history of South Asia. It was a time of profound loss and upheaval, yet it also paved the way for the emergence of two sovereign nations, each with its own vision for the future. The journey from colonial subjugation to independence—and from the agony of partition to the hope of nation-building—stands as a powerful reminder of the capacity for renewal even in the wake of deep historical trauma. The legacy of partition endures, compelling us to remember that the birth of modern nations is a story of both sorrow and hope, of endings that sow the seeds for new beginnings.

9

Building a Republic – India's Post-Colonial Transformation

Emerging from the tumultuous era of partition and colonial rule, India embarked on an ambitious journey of self-governance and national reconstruction. The birth of the Republic of India marked not only political independence but also a radical transformation of society, economy, and culture. In this chapter, we trace the evolution of post-colonial India, from the framing of a unique constitutional order to the sweeping socio-economic reforms that have defined the nation's modern trajectory. Drawing on works such as Jawaharlal Nehru's *The Discovery of India*, Granville Austin's *The Indian Constitution: Cornerstone of a Nation*, and Amartya Sen's *Development as Freedom*, we explore how India endeavored to reconcile its ancient traditions with the imperatives of modernity.

The Birth of a New Political Order

The Constitution: Blueprint of a Nation

At the heart of India's post-colonial transformation lies the Constitution, a document that sought to balance diverse interests, forge unity in diversity, and set the stage for democratic governance. Drafted between 1947 and 1950, the Constitution of India was a monumental task that involved reconciling centuries-old traditions with the ideals of equality, liberty, and social justice. Led by Dr. B.R. Ambedkar and a group of visionary leaders, the Constituent Assembly worked tirelessly to craft a framework that would reflect the aspirations of a newly independent nation.

Granville Austin, in *The Indian Constitution: Cornerstone of a Nation*, details how the framers of the Constitution envisioned it as not merely a legal document but a social contract—a promise to secure the rights of every citizen regardless of caste, creed, or gender. The document enshrines a commitment to secularism, democracy, and federalism, providing the legal scaffolding for a pluralistic society. The elaborate preamble, which declares India a sovereign, socialist, secular, democratic republic, encapsulates the nation's desire to leave behind the divisions and inequities of the colonial past.

Democratic Institutions and Federal Structure

The adoption of the Constitution in 1950 heralded the establishment of a democratic system that was unprecedented in its scale and complexity. India's vast and diverse population was integrated into a federal system, with power divided between the central government and the states. This structure was critical for accommodating regional identities and ensuring that local issues received attention alongside national concerns.

The democratic experiment in India was characterized by free and fair elections, a vibrant multiparty system, and an independent judiciary that played a crucial role in upholding constitutional rights. In *The Discovery of India*, Jawaharlal Nehru reflects on the challenges of nation-building and the central role that democratic institutions were expected to play in nurturing a sense of national unity. Over the decades, India has held numerous elections, reinforcing the legitimacy of its political system even as it has evolved to meet new challenges.

Economic Transformation and the Quest for Development

Industrialization and Economic Planning

Post-independence India faced the enormous task of rebuilding an economy that had been systematically reoriented to serve colonial interests. The economic policies adopted by the newly formed government were aimed at achieving self-sufficiency, reducing poverty, and fostering industrial growth. Guided by the principles of planned development, successive governments set up the Planning Commission and introduced a series of Five-Year Plans to direct investment and allocate resources strategically.

Amartya Sen, in *Development as Freedom*, argues that India's focus on inclusive growth—emphasizing both economic and social dimensions of development—was essential for transforming a society deeply scarred by colonial exploitation. The early plans prioritized heavy industries, infrastructure development, and the modernization of agriculture, all intended to create a robust industrial base and lift millions out of poverty. Despite challenges such as bureaucratic inefficiencies and resource constraints, these initiatives laid the foundation for a more self-reliant economy.

Liberalization and Global Integration

By the late 20th century, however, it became clear that India's socialist-inspired economic policies were not sufficient to fully unlock its potential. In response to stagnating growth and mounting economic pressures, the government initiated a series of sweeping economic reforms in the early 1990s. Liberalization, privatization, and globalization marked a paradigm shift—opening up the economy to foreign investment, deregulating key industries, and encouraging entrepreneurship.

These reforms, detailed in numerous economic studies, catalyzed rapid growth, transformed the industrial landscape, and integrated India more deeply into the global economy. While critics point to increased inequality and regional disparities, the overall impact has been significant, with millions of Indians lifting themselves into new economic opportunities. The transformation of India into one of the world's fastest-growing economies stands as a testament to the resilience and adaptability of its post-colonial vision.

Social Reforms and Cultural Renaissance

Addressing Caste, Gender, and Inequality

Alongside economic development, India's post-colonial transformation has been deeply marked by efforts to address historical social inequities. The legacy of centuries of caste discrimination, gender biases, and social stratification posed enormous challenges to creating a truly egalitarian society. Recognizing this, the framers of the Constitution enshrined a number of progressive measures, including affirmative action policies, reservations in education and employment, and legal safeguards for women and marginalized communities.

In *The Discovery of India*, Nehru emphasized that political freedom must be accompanied by social freedom. Subsequent governments have worked to implement policies designed to redress historical injustices and promote social inclusion. Landmark legislation, such as the Hindu Code Bills and various anti-discrimination laws, has gradually altered the social fabric, challenging entrenched prejudices and opening new pathways for social mobility. Although significant challenges remain, the ongoing struggle for social justice continues to shape public discourse and policy in contemporary India.

Education, Science, and Technological Advancement

A key pillar of India's post-colonial transformation has been the emphasis on education and scientific research. The establishment of institutions such as the Indian Institutes of Technology (IITs) and the Indian Institutes of Management (IIMs) has propelled India to the forefront of technological innovation and research. These institutions, along with an expanding network of universities and research centers, have nurtured generations of scientists, engineers, and thinkers who have driven the nation's modern advancements.

Educational reforms have also played a pivotal role in democratizing knowledge and empowering citizens. As Amartya Sen discusses in *Development as Freedom*, education is not merely a tool for economic progress but a means of enhancing individual capabilities and expanding the boundaries of human freedom. The proliferation of higher education and research has contributed to a vibrant intellectual culture, laying the groundwork for India's emergence as a global player in fields ranging from information technology to biotechnology.

Cultural Reawakening and National Identity

The post-independence period has witnessed a cultural renaissance that sought to reclaim India's rich heritage while embracing the innovations of the modern era. This period saw the revitalization of Indian literature, music, cinema, and the arts, blending traditional motifs with contemporary sensibilities. Indian cinema, in particular, emerged as a powerful medium for storytelling and cultural expression, reaching audiences both domestically and globally.

Writers, artists, and intellectuals began to explore themes of identity, freedom, and the complexities of modern life. This cultural reawakening was not merely a revival of past glories but a dynamic process that reflected the evolving realities of a diverse, modern nation. In works such as *The Argumentative Indian* by Amartya Sen, the interplay between tradition and modernity is examined, highlighting how India's pluralistic heritage continues to influence its creative expressions. The result has been a vibrant cultural landscape that not only preserves ancient traditions but also continuously reinvents them in dialogue with global trends.

Political Challenges and the Evolution of Democracy

Navigating Regional and Ethnic Diversity

India's democratic journey has been characterized by the delicate balancing act of managing regional, linguistic, and ethnic diversity. The federal structure enshrined in the Constitution has provided a framework for accommodating regional aspirations while maintaining national unity. However, the tension between central authority and regional identities has occasionally led to political challenges, including demands for greater autonomy and, in some cases, secessionist movements.

The evolution of India's political system, as described in Granville Austin's *The Indian Constitution: Cornerstone of a Nation*, demonstrates how democratic institutions have been tested and, over time, strengthened through ongoing dialogue and reform. Political leaders at both the national and state levels have had to negotiate the complexities of a diverse society, ensuring that the voices of minority communities and regional groups are represented. Despite occasional setbacks, India's commitment to democratic principles has allowed it to absorb and adapt to these challenges, continually reaffirming its status as the world's largest democracy.

Economic Disparities and Social Justice

One of the enduring challenges for post-colonial India has been addressing economic disparities that continue to reflect historical legacies. While economic liberalization has spurred growth and innovation, the benefits have not been uniformly distributed. Rural areas, in particular, have struggled with underdevelopment, limited access to education and healthcare, and infrastructural deficits.

In response, successive governments have launched initiatives aimed at reducing poverty and promoting rural development. Programs focused on land reform, rural electrification, and microfinance have sought to empower marginalized communities and foster inclusive growth. The discourse on economic justice, as articulated by Amartya Sen and other scholars, emphasizes that true development must be measured not solely by GDP growth but by the expansion of human freedoms and capabilities. The pursuit of social justice continues to be a defining feature of India's democratic ethos, shaping policy debates and public priorities.

Reflections on the Journey So Far

The Legacy of Visionary Leadership

The post-colonial transformation of India is inseparable from the vision and leadership of its founding figures. Leaders like Jawaharlal Nehru, Sardar Patel, and Dr. B.R. Ambedkar played critical roles in charting a course for the nation—a course that balanced modernity with tradition, unity with diversity, and economic development with social justice. Their writings and speeches continue to inspire new generations, serving as touchstones for the ongoing quest to realize India's democratic and developmental ideals.

Nehru's *The Discovery of India* remains a seminal work that captures the spirit of a nation reborn—a nation striving to reconcile its ancient past with the demands of modernity. The ideals articulated by these visionaries continue to guide policy debates and shape the national narrative, reminding citizens that the journey toward a more just and equitable society is both an inherited responsibility and an ongoing endeavor.

Ongoing Challenges and Future Aspirations

While India has made tremendous strides in building a republic that is both democratic and dynamic, the path forward is fraught with challenges. Economic inequality, regional disparities, and social tensions continue to test the resilience of its institutions. Environmental concerns, technological disruptions, and the pressures of global integration add further layers of complexity to the nation's developmental trajectory.

Yet, the same spirit of innovation and adaptation that has characterized India's post-colonial transformation offers hope for the future. The robust debate over policy, the vibrancy of its civil society, and the dynamism of its democratic institutions suggest that India remains committed to the ideals of freedom, justice, and inclusive growth. As the nation looks to the future, its leaders and citizens are tasked with navigating the delicate balance between tradition and modernity, ensuring that the gains of independence continue to benefit all segments of society.

Concluding Thoughts

The journey from colonial subjugation to a sovereign, democratic republic is a saga of immense challenges and remarkable achievements. India's post-colonial transformation—a process marked by the drafting of an inclusive Constitution, ambitious economic planning, bold social reforms, and a vibrant cultural renaissance—stands as a testament to the nation's enduring resilience and vision. As we reflect on this transformative era, the insights provided by Nehru in *The Discovery of India*, Granville Austin's detailed analyses, and Amartya Sen's reflections on development serve as enduring reminders of the ideals that continue to shape modern India.

In the years since independence, India has striven to create a society that honors its diverse heritage while embracing the opportunities of a globalized world. The republic that emerged in 1950 was not merely a political construct but a living, evolving experiment in democracy—a project that, despite its challenges, has continually sought to empower its citizens and expand the boundaries of freedom. The journey is far from complete, but each step forward is built upon the foundation laid by those who dared to dream of a new India.

As we look ahead, the legacy of India's post-colonial transformation invites us to reaffirm our commitment to democratic values, social justice, and economic progress. It challenges us to build on the achievements of the past, to address the inequalities that remain, and to forge a future where the aspirations of every citizen can be realized. In doing so, we honor not only the vision of India's founding leaders but also the enduring spirit of a nation that continues to reinvent itself in pursuit of a more equitable and prosperous tomorrow.

For those wishing to delve further into this rich history, key texts such as *The Discovery of India* by Jawaharlal Nehru, *The Indian Constitution: Cornerstone of a Nation* by Granville Austin, and *Development as Freedom* by Amartya Sen provide invaluable insights into the myriad dimensions of India's post-colonial transformation. These works, among others, illuminate the challenges and triumphs of building a republic—a story that remains as relevant today as it was in the formative years of independence.

In sum, the building of the Indian republic is a saga of determination and renewal. It is a story that weaves together the threads of constitutional innovation, economic planning, social reform, and cultural revival into a tapestry that continues to inspire future generations. As India moves forward, the lessons of its post-colonial journey remain vital—a beacon guiding the nation towards a future defined by justice, unity, and sustained progress.

10

Unity in Diversity – Culture, Languages, and Regional Identities

India's strength has long been celebrated not as a nation of uniformity, but as a living mosaic of cultures, languages, and traditions. This chapter explores the ways in which India's astounding diversity has been both a challenge and a source of immense creative energy, ultimately forging a unique national identity. Drawing on scholarly works such as John Keay's *India: A History*, Amartya Sen's *The Argumentative Indian*, and Romila Thapar's *Early India: From the Origins to AD 1300*, we examine how centuries of pluralistic interaction have shaped India's political, social, and cultural landscape, and how this "unity in diversity" has become a central pillar of modern Indian identity.

A Tapestry of Cultures and Traditions

Historical Roots of Pluralism

India's historical narrative is a story of layers and interwoven threads—each culture, language, and tradition contributes to a complex and vibrant fabric. From the earliest civilizations of the Indus Valley to the Vedic period, ancient India witnessed an influx of ideas and peoples. As Romila Thapar explains in *Early India: From the Origins to AD 1300*, this era laid the foundation for a cultural synthesis where indigenous practices and external influences began to merge, setting the stage for centuries of pluralistic evolution.

The subcontinent's geographical diversity—spanning mountains, deserts, and fertile plains—helped nurture distinct regional identities that developed their own customs, dialects, and ways of life. Over time, the arrival of various empires, from the Mauryas and Guptas to the Mughals and British, further enriched this pluralism. Each ruling dynasty brought with it new artistic, religious, and administrative practices that blended with local traditions. This dynamic exchange contributed to a shared sense of cultural continuity despite regional differences—a phenomenon often described as the "unity in diversity" that remains central to the Indian ethos.

Regional Traditions and Their Contributions

India is not a monolith; its regions tell unique stories. For example, the classical arts of South India—ranging from Carnatic music to Bharatanatyam dance—have developed over centuries and continue to flourish as symbols of cultural pride. In the north, traditions such as Hindustani classical music and the rich heritage of Mughal art have influenced the aesthetics of a diverse populace. Even within the vast linguistic spectrum, languages like Hindi, Bengali, Tamil, Marathi, and many others have cultivated distinct literary and cultural traditions while contributing to a national narrative.

John Keay, in *India: A History*, emphasizes that while these regional identities have evolved independently, they have also engaged in constant dialogue with one another through trade, migration, and shared religious practices. This continuous interchange has allowed India to maintain internal cohesion even as its regions retain their unique characteristics. The synthesis of diverse traditions has resulted in a cultural mosaic that is both resilient and adaptive—a mosaic that continues to evolve with each generation.

The Role of Religion and Philosophy

Spiritual Plurality as a Unifying Force

Religion in India has historically been a major force for both unity and diversity. The subcontinent is the birthplace of major world religions, including Hinduism, Buddhism, Jainism, and Sikhism. Each of these traditions contributes its own philosophical depth, rituals, and cultural practices, yet they often share common ethical and metaphysical themes. This pluralistic religious landscape has fostered an environment where debate and dialogue are not only accepted but celebrated. As Amartya Sen discusses in *The Argumentative Indian*, the tradition of public reasoning and debate over ideas has been a hallmark of Indian civilization, enabling a vibrant exchange of thoughts that transcends sectarian boundaries.

Furthermore, the syncretic tendencies of Indian spirituality—

evident in movements such as Sufism and the Bhakti tradition—demonstrate the country's capacity to blend disparate ideas into a harmonious whole. Sufi mystics, for instance, often embraced the devotional practices of Hinduism, while Bhakti poets in regions like Maharashtra and Tamil Nadu infused local languages with universal themes of love and devotion. These interreligious dialogues not only enriched the cultural life of the nation but also helped to soften communal tensions by highlighting common human aspirations.

Philosophical Contributions and Intellectual Traditions

The intellectual tradition of India is equally diverse and robust. Ancient texts like the Upanishads and later works of classical Sanskrit literature have provided philosophical frameworks that continue to influence modern thought. Indian philosophy has engaged with questions of existence, morality, and the nature of the universe in ways that are remarkably inclusive. Philosophers and scholars have long argued that the strength of Indian thought lies in its capacity to accommodate contradictions and embrace multiplicity—an approach that mirrors the broader societal mosaic.

The legacy of intellectual pluralism is well captured in Amartya Sen's *The Argumentative Indian*, which illustrates how the tradition of debate and discussion has fostered a culture of dissent and critical inquiry. This tradition is not confined to academia; it permeates the public sphere, where diverse opinions coexist and contribute to a dynamic democratic process. Such intellectual resilience has helped India navigate the complexities of modernity while remaining rooted in its historical and cultural traditions.

Linguistic Diversity: A Vital Component of National Identity

The Rich Spectrum of Indian Languages

Language is one of the most visible markers of India's diversity. The country is home to hundreds of languages and dialects, many of which have rich literary traditions spanning centuries. Sanskrit, Tamil, Bengali, Marathi, Punjabi, and many others each carry their own literary canons and cultural heritages. Despite the linguistic diversity, modern India has managed to forge a sense of national unity through the adoption of Hindi and English as official languages, along with the promotion of multilingual education and media.

Efforts to preserve and promote linguistic diversity have been central to post-colonial policies. The Indian Constitution recognizes the importance of regional languages and provides for their development and protection. This policy framework acknowledges that language is not only a means of communication but also an expression of cultural identity. The celebration of linguistic festivals, the translation of classic works into multiple languages, and the vibrant film industries in various regional languages all underscore the pluralistic spirit of Indian society.

The Politics of Language and Identity

Language has also been a political issue in India, often serving as a flashpoint for regional aspirations and tensions. The reorganization of states along linguistic lines in the 1950s is a testament to the power of language as a marker of identity. This process, while at times contentious, ultimately aimed to create administrative units that could better address the cultural and economic needs of their populations.

Scholars like Dilip Hiro have argued that the linguistic reorganization of states contributed significantly to political stability by aligning administrative boundaries with cultural and linguistic realities. This approach has allowed for greater local autonomy and has helped to mitigate conflicts by ensuring that diverse linguistic groups have a say in their governance. The ongoing debate over language policy in India reflects a broader commitment to respecting diversity while fostering national unity—a balancing act that remains central to the country's democratic ethos.

Cultural Festivals and Shared Celebrations

Festivals as Expressions of Unity

Cultural festivals in India offer a vivid illustration of unity in diversity. Celebrations such as Diwali, Eid, Christmas, Navratri, and Pongal—along with countless regional and local festivals—demonstrate how religious and cultural diversity can coexist harmoniously. These festivals are not merely religious observances; they are vibrant expressions of cultural identity that bring people together regardless of their background.

For instance, Diwali, the festival of lights, is celebrated by millions of Hindus, Sikhs, and even some Buddhists, each adding their own regional flavor to the festivities. Similarly, Eid is celebrated with equal fervor across different communities, fostering a sense of shared joy and communal solidarity. The mutual participation in each other's festivals has helped to bridge communal divides and foster a sense of belonging that transcends narrow identities.

In his work *India: A History*, John Keay highlights how such celebrations have long been a source of national integration, offering a space where diverse traditions converge in celebration of life and community. The cultural practice of sharing festive foods, music, dance, and rituals creates bonds that contribute to the overarching narrative of a unified yet diverse India.

Culinary Diversity and Shared Heritage

Another striking example of India's unity in diversity is found in its culinary traditions. Indian cuisine is a melting pot of influences—spices, cooking techniques, and ingredients vary widely from region to region, yet together they create a cohesive gastronomic tapestry. Whether it is the rich, aromatic curries of the north, the tangy, coconut-infused dishes of the south, or the delectable street foods of the west and east, each culinary tradition adds to the nation's shared cultural heritage.

Food, like language and art, becomes a medium for cultural expression and exchange. Shared culinary practices have often served as a bridge between communities, fostering cross-cultural interactions and mutual appreciation. This culinary diversity not only celebrates regional uniqueness but also contributes to a collective identity that is unmistakably Indian.

Contemporary Reflections on Diversity

Modern Challenges and Opportunities

In modern India, the challenge of balancing unity and diversity continues to be both a political and social endeavor. Rapid urbanization, globalization, and technological advances have introduced new dynamics into the cultural landscape. On one hand, these forces have created opportunities for greater integration, communication, and economic development. On the other, they have sometimes amplified regional and linguistic divides, as local identities assert themselves in the face of homogenizing global influences.

Political debates over language policy, regional autonomy, and cultural preservation remain central to contemporary discourse. The federal structure of India, with its built-in mechanisms for regional representation, has helped to address some of these issues. However, the ongoing challenge is to ensure that diversity is celebrated without fragmenting the nation's collective identity.

The Role of Education and Media

Education and media play crucial roles in shaping perceptions of unity and diversity. School curricula that incorporate regional histories and languages, along with national narratives, help foster an appreciation of India's pluralistic heritage from a young age. Likewise, the media—both traditional and digital—has the power to highlight stories of cultural convergence, shared traditions, and the everyday interactions that knit together the social fabric.

In *The Argumentative Indian*, Amartya Sen emphasizes that a healthy democracy thrives on robust debate and the exchange of ideas, a process that is enriched by exposure to diverse perspectives. Media representations that celebrate cultural differences while emphasizing common values contribute to a more inclusive national identity. The challenge for modern India is to harness the power of education and media to promote a vision of unity that does not erase regional distinctions but rather integrates them into a larger narrative of progress and mutual respect.

Reimagining National Identity: The Way Forward

Embracing Pluralism in Policy and Practice

The future of India's national identity lies in embracing its diversity as a strength rather than a source of division. Policymakers and civic leaders continue to explore ways to ensure that economic, social, and cultural development benefits all segments of society. Inclusive policies—whether in education, healthcare, or economic planning—must recognize and respect the pluralistic nature of the nation.

Efforts to promote multilingualism, preserve regional art forms, and celebrate cultural festivals are essential components of a broader strategy to build a cohesive society. The successes and challenges of these initiatives are chronicled in various scholarly works, which collectively suggest that the Indian model of unity in diversity, though complex and sometimes fraught, offers valuable lessons for the world.

Global Implications of India's Model

India's experiment with diversity has global resonance. In an increasingly interconnected world, the ability to manage pluralism and foster dialogue among disparate groups is a quality that many nations aspire to emulate. The Indian experience demonstrates that unity does not require uniformity, and that a nation can be both diverse and united. This lesson is particularly relevant in today's globalized environment, where cultural, religious, and linguistic differences are often sources of conflict rather than cooperation.

As contemporary scholars reflect on India's journey, works like John Keay's *India: A History* and Amartya Sen's *The Argumentative Indian* remind us that the nation's resilience and dynamism are rooted in its pluralism. The success of India's democratic experiment—and its ability to create a vibrant, inclusive society—offers a model for addressing similar challenges elsewhere in the world.

Concluding Reflections

The idea of unity in diversity has been a constant, albeit evolving, theme throughout India's history. From ancient times through medieval and colonial periods to the present day, the ability to weave together a multitude of languages, religions, cultures, and traditions has defined the Indian experience. While this diversity presents challenges, it has also been the source of profound strength and creativity.

As we reflect on the cultural, linguistic, and regional dimensions of India's identity, it becomes clear that the nation's pluralism is not a weakness but a vibrant asset—a testament to centuries of intercultural exchange and the enduring human spirit. The integration of diverse traditions into a coherent national narrative is an ongoing project, one that requires continual dialogue, innovative policymaking, and a commitment to celebrating differences while forging common bonds.

In envisioning the future, India's path forward lies in nurturing this pluralistic heritage and ensuring that every community feels valued and heard. The stories of everyday life—from the shared joy of a festival to the collaborative spirit of local governance—speak to a national ethos that is inclusive and dynamic. This ethos, captured so eloquently in works such as *The Argumentative Indian* by Amartya Sen, continues to inspire new generations to build a society that honors its diverse past while striving for a united, progressive future.

For readers seeking a deeper understanding of India's rich tapestry of cultures and languages, key texts such as John Keay's *India: A History*, Amartya Sen's *The Argumentative Indian*, and Romila Thapar's *Early India: From the Origins to AD 1300* provide invaluable insights. These works offer complementary perspectives that illuminate how diversity has not only shaped India's history but also continues to be a driving force in its development.

In conclusion, the story of India's unity in diversity is one of resilience, creativity, and hope—a narrative that underscores the belief that strength comes not from uniformity, but from the ability to embrace and integrate differences. As India moves forward into the future, its vibrant mosaic of cultures, languages, and identities will remain its greatest asset, inspiring a nation to continue its journey toward a more inclusive and harmonious society.

11

Contemporary India – Challenges, Triumphs, and Global Aspirations

In recent decades, India has emerged as one of the most dynamic and rapidly changing societies in the world. The nation now stands at a crossroads where a rich historical legacy converges with rapid modernization, technological innovation, and evolving global aspirations. This chapter explores the multifaceted landscape of contemporary India by examining its economic progress, social challenges, political transformations, and international role. Drawing on works such as Ramachandra Guha's *India After Gandhi*, Edward Luce's *In Spite of the Gods: The Rise of Modern India*, and John Keay's *India: A History*, we analyze how India is negotiating its path forward in a rapidly changing global environment.

Economic Dynamism and Transformation

The Rise of a Global Economic Power

India's economic journey in the post-liberalization era has been nothing short of remarkable. Since the economic reforms of the early 1990s, the country has transitioned from a predominantly agrarian economy to one that is increasingly service-oriented and technology-driven. These reforms spurred unprecedented growth rates and created a burgeoning middle class that has fueled domestic consumption and innovation.

Edward Luce, in *In Spite of the Gods*, outlines how liberalization opened up new markets, attracted foreign investments, and led to the expansion of sectors like information technology, telecommunications, and pharmaceuticals. Indian companies have not only become key players in global markets but have also driven homegrown innovation that is tailored to local needs. Today, cities like Bangalore, Hyderabad, and Pune are recognized worldwide as hubs of technological advancement and start-up culture.

Challenges in Economic Equity and Inclusive Growth

Despite these triumphs, economic disparities persist. While urban centers have flourished, rural areas continue to struggle with inadequate infrastructure, limited access to healthcare, and education disparities. The challenge of ensuring that the benefits of rapid economic growth are equitably shared remains a critical issue for policymakers. Ramachandra Guha's *India After Gandhi* highlights how the legacy of colonial resource extraction and subsequent economic policies have contributed to regional and social inequalities that persist even today.

Government initiatives aimed at improving rural development, such as the Mahatma Gandhi National Rural Employment Guarantee Act (MGNREGA) and various agricultural reforms, are designed to bridge these gaps. Yet, balancing rapid modernization with inclusive development continues to be an ongoing and complex challenge that demands innovative policy solutions and sustained political will.

Social and Cultural Evolution

Demographic Shifts and Urbanization

India's demographic profile is a key driver of its contemporary transformation. With a population exceeding 1.3 billion, India is home to the world's largest youth demographic—a potent force for social and economic change. Rapid urbanization has led to the growth of mega-cities that are hubs of cultural and economic activity. However, this urban explosion has also presented challenges, including housing shortages, environmental degradation, and strained public services.

Urban planning initiatives and smart-city projects are underway in many parts of the country to address these issues. Yet, the pace of urbanization often outstrips the development of essential infrastructure, leading to persistent challenges such as traffic congestion, pollution, and inequitable access to resources. These problems are intricately linked with the broader narrative of India's transformation, where the promise of progress must be reconciled with sustainable and inclusive urban development.

The Evolving Social Fabric

Contemporary India is also witnessing significant changes in its social fabric. Traditional social hierarchies, including those based on caste and gender, are being increasingly challenged by a more assertive middle class and growing social awareness. The rise of digital media and social networking has created platforms for marginalized voices and fostered debates around social justice, equality, and human rights.

Works like *The Argumentative Indian* by Amartya Sen illustrate how the long tradition of public discourse and intellectual debate in India is being revitalized in the modern era. From campaigns against gender discrimination to movements advocating for the rights of lower castes and indigenous communities, the struggle for social justice continues to be a defining feature of contemporary Indian society. This ongoing evolution is reshaping cultural norms and contributing to a more inclusive public sphere.

Political Landscape and Democratic Resilience

Strengthening of Democratic Institutions

Since independence, India has sustained its reputation as the world's largest democracy. Over the decades, democratic institutions have been tested by political volatility, corruption scandals, and regional tensions, yet the resilience of India's democratic framework has often surprised both insiders and external observers. Free and fair elections, a robust judicial system, and a vibrant civil society have all played a role in maintaining democratic continuity even during turbulent periods.

In *India After Gandhi*, Ramachandra Guha documents how democratic practices have not only survived but evolved, becoming more participatory and representative. The dynamic interplay between central and state governments, despite occasional friction, has ensured that diverse regional voices are heard within the larger national discourse. However, challenges such as populism, political polarization, and concerns over freedom of the press continue to necessitate ongoing vigilance and reform.

The Role of Regional Politics

Regional politics in India have also taken on increased significance in shaping national policy and discourse. The federal structure of India, enshrined in its Constitution, allows for a degree of regional autonomy that has been crucial in managing the country's diversity. Political parties with regional bases have emerged as influential players in both state and national elections, advocating for local issues and cultural identities while also contributing to broader debates on national development.

The tension between regional aspirations and national integration is an ongoing feature of India's political life. While regional movements have sometimes led to demands for greater autonomy or even secessionist sentiments, they have also enriched the national conversation by bringing unique perspectives and localized policy innovations to the forefront. This balance of power between regional and national interests is both a challenge and a strength, as it forces constant negotiation and adaptation within India's evolving democracy.

India's Global Aspirations

Repositioning on the World Stage

In the 21st century, India's transformation is not confined to its internal dynamics; it is also redefining its role in the global arena. The nation's rapid economic growth, technological prowess, and expanding military capabilities have positioned it as an emerging global power. Diplomatic initiatives such as the "Act East" policy and increased participation in international organizations underscore India's ambitions to shape regional and global affairs.

In *In Spite of the Gods*, Edward Luce argues that India's rise is not merely an economic phenomenon but also a geopolitical shift that has significant implications for global politics. As India navigates complex relationships with traditional powers like the United States, China, and Russia, it is also actively engaging with neighboring countries through regional forums such as the South Asian Association for Regional Cooperation (SAARC) and the Bay of Bengal Initiative for Multi-Sectoral Technical and Economic Cooperation (BIMSTEC).

Soft Power and Cultural Diplomacy

Beyond its economic and military might, India is also leveraging its rich cultural heritage as a form of soft power. The global appeal of Bollywood, yoga, cuisine, and literature has helped shape a positive international image. Cultural diplomacy initiatives, including international film festivals, art exhibitions, and academic exchanges, have contributed to a broader understanding of India's multifaceted identity. These cultural exports serve as a bridge between India's ancient traditions and its modern aspirations, enhancing its influence on the world stage.

John Keay's *India: A History* offers valuable insights into how India's historical legacy of cultural synthesis and pluralism continues to inform its contemporary global identity. The international popularity of Indian cultural forms reinforces the idea that diversity and inclusivity are not only internal assets but also key elements of India's global brand.

Technological Innovation and Environmental Challenges

The Digital Revolution

One of the most striking features of contemporary India is its digital revolution. The widespread adoption of smartphones, high-speed internet, and digital payment systems has transformed everyday life in India. Initiatives like "Digital India" have sought to extend connectivity to rural and underserved areas, bridging the digital divide and creating new opportunities for education, commerce, and governance.

This technological surge has spurred innovation in fields ranging from information technology and biotechnology to renewable energy and space exploration. Indian start-ups and tech giants alike are now recognized as significant contributors to the global digital economy. The rapid pace of technological change is not without its challenges, however. Issues related to data privacy, cybersecurity, and the equitable distribution of digital resources remain at the forefront of public policy debates.

Balancing Growth and Sustainability

As India continues its journey of rapid industrialization and urbanization, environmental concerns have become increasingly urgent. Air and water pollution, deforestation, and the impacts of climate change pose significant risks to public health and economic sustainability. The government, in collaboration with non-governmental organizations and international agencies, has launched initiatives aimed at promoting sustainable development and mitigating environmental degradation.

Efforts to expand renewable energy capacity, such as solar and wind power projects, are critical components of India's strategy to balance economic growth with environmental stewardship. Scholars like Amartya Sen have stressed that true development must account for the long-term health of both society and the environment—a lesson that is particularly pertinent in the context of India's rapid modernization. The challenge for contemporary India is to innovate in ways that are both economically beneficial and ecologically responsible.

Reflections on Contemporary India

Triumphs and Ongoing Struggles

Contemporary India is a nation of contrasts—a country where extraordinary achievements coexist with persistent challenges. On one hand, India's economic rise, technological progress, and vibrant democratic culture have generated optimism about its future. On the other, issues such as social inequality, environmental degradation, and political polarization continue to demand attention and reform.

The intellectual and cultural debates that characterize modern India reflect an ongoing engagement with the nation's complex past and an ambitious vision for the future. As Ramachandra Guha's *India After Gandhi* and other seminal works illustrate, the story of modern India is not one of linear progress but of continuous negotiation between tradition and innovation, unity and diversity, aspiration and reality.

The Role of Citizens in Shaping the Future

At the heart of India's contemporary transformation lies the active engagement of its citizens. The democratization of information through digital media, the rise of social movements advocating for justice and equality, and the increasing participation of youth in public discourse are all indicators of a society in vibrant flux. The power of collective action, whether through grassroots mobilization or civic engagement, underscores the belief that the future of India will be determined not solely by its leaders but by the everyday contributions of millions of citizens.

As India charts its course into the future, its ability to harness the energy of its diverse population and to build bridges between competing interests will be crucial. The lessons of India's long history—its resilience in the face of adversity, its capacity for reinvention, and its commitment to pluralism—offer hope that the challenges of the present can be transformed into opportunities for sustainable progress.

Concluding Thoughts

India's contemporary journey is a testament to the enduring spirit of a nation that has weathered centuries of change. From its economic dynamism and technological innovation to its complex social fabric and vibrant democratic culture, modern India embodies both the triumphs of progress and the challenges of maintaining unity in a diverse and rapidly evolving landscape.

In reflecting on the multifaceted story of contemporary India, we are reminded that its success lies not in uniformity but in the ability to integrate diverse ideas, cultures, and aspirations into a cohesive whole. As India continues to engage with the global community—whether through economic partnerships, cultural diplomacy, or technological collaboration—the lessons of its past remain vital. Seminal works such as Ramachandra Guha's *India After Gandhi*, Edward Luce's *In Spite of the Gods*, and John Keay's *India: A History* offer deep insights into the forces that have shaped modern India and continue to guide its future.

Ultimately, the story of contemporary India is one of transformation and hope—a journey that exemplifies the power of resilience, innovation, and collective vision. As the nation moves forward into an increasingly interconnected world, the challenges it faces will be met with the same spirit of ingenuity and determination that has defined its history. In doing so, India not only honors its past but also lays the groundwork for a future characterized by justice, sustainability, and inclusive progress—a future that remains open to the aspirations of every citizen and the promise of a nation united in diversity.

For those seeking further understanding of these dynamic changes, key texts such as *India After Gandhi* by Ramachandra Guha, *In Spite of the Gods* by Edward Luce, and *India: A History* by

John Keay provide comprehensive perspectives on the journey of modern India. These works underscore that while challenges persist, the ongoing transformation of India is a powerful narrative of hope, resilience, and the potential for a brighter tomorrow.

In summary, contemporary India is a nation in constant evolution—a mosaic of triumphs and challenges that continues to redefine what it means to be Indian in the 21st century. Its journey offers profound lessons not only for its own citizens but also for the global community, as it illustrates how diversity, when embraced and nurtured, can become a cornerstone of progress and a beacon of inspiration for the world.

12

Reflections and the Road Ahead – India's Journey into the Future

As we conclude this exploration of India's vast historical canvas, we turn our gaze toward the horizon to examine the future of a nation that has long thrived on its capacity for reinvention. In this final chapter, we reflect on the lessons of the past, evaluate the challenges and opportunities of the present, and chart possible trajectories for India's future. Drawing on insights from Ramachandra Guha's India After Gandhi, Amartya Sen's Development as Freedom, and John Keay's India: A History, among others, we consider how India's enduring spirit of resilience, diversity, and innovation can guide it as it navigates the uncertainties of the 21st century.

Learning from the Past

Historical Resilience as a Beacon for Tomorrow

India's history is a story of constant transformation. From the ancient urban centers of the Indus Valley to the intellectual ferment of the Vedic age, from the grandeur of the Maurya and Gupta empires to the cultural synthesis of the Mughal period, and later, the crucible of colonialism and the long struggle for freedom—each era has left an indelible mark on the nation's identity. Historians like John Keay, in *India: A History*, remind us that India's ability to absorb and transform external influences has been its greatest strength. Today, as India faces the challenges of rapid modernization and globalization, the lessons of historical resilience offer both inspiration and guidance.

The past teaches that transformation, while often painful, can lead to renewed strength. Ramachandra Guha, in *India After Gandhi*, underscores that the collective memory of overcoming adversity is embedded in the national psyche. This deep-rooted sense of endurance continues to inspire new generations to push forward despite setbacks, suggesting that India's future may well be defined by its capacity to learn from history and innovate for tomorrow.

Embracing Pluralism and Inclusive Progress

One of the enduring themes of Indian history is its pluralism. The very concept of "unity in diversity" has been a cornerstone of Indian society—from the syncretic spiritual traditions of the medieval era to the democratic framework that emerged post-independence. Amartya Sen's *The Argumentative Indian* offers a compelling analysis of how debate, dialogue, and pluralism have always driven intellectual and cultural progress in India. In envisioning its future, India's strength will continue to reside in its ability to accommodate differences and build consensus across varied communities.

As India advances, policies that foster inclusive growth and protect cultural diversity will be crucial. Whether addressing the challenges of economic inequality or integrating diverse regional identities, the nation's future depends on the effective translation of its pluralistic ideals into everyday governance and social practice.

Navigating Contemporary Challenges

Economic Inequality and Sustainable Development

India's rapid economic growth over the past few decades is a cause for celebration. The nation has emerged as a global economic power, buoyed by a robust technology sector, burgeoning entrepreneurship, and an ever-expanding middle class. However, this progress has been accompanied by significant challenges. Persistent economic disparities, both between urban and rural areas and among different social groups, threaten to undermine the promise of inclusive development.

Amartya Sen, in *Development as Freedom*, argues that true progress must be measured not only in terms of GDP growth but also by the extent to which economic gains are shared equitably across society. Addressing these disparities will require a multi-pronged strategy: investment in rural infrastructure, reforms in education and healthcare, and targeted social policies that empower marginalized communities. The future of India may well hinge on its ability to reconcile the demands of rapid modernization with the imperative of social justice.

Environmental Sustainability in a Changing World

Another major challenge facing contemporary India is environmental sustainability. As the nation continues to industrialize and urbanize at an unprecedented pace, environmental degradation, air and water pollution, and the impacts of climate change have become critical issues. The health of the nation's natural resources is inextricably linked to the quality of life for its citizens, making sustainable development a priority for the future.

Innovative solutions are emerging to address these challenges. Government initiatives to expand renewable energy sources, such as solar and wind power, along with efforts to improve waste management and water conservation, reflect a growing awareness of the need for ecological balance. Yet, achieving a sustainable future will require the integration of environmental considerations into all aspects of policy and development. Visionary leadership and a commitment to long-term planning, as discussed in Edward Luce's *In Spite of the Gods: The Rise of Modern India*, will be essential in steering India toward a greener, more sustainable path.

Technological Innovation and the Digital Divide

India's digital revolution is transforming society in profound ways. The proliferation of smartphones, high-speed internet, and digital payment systems has unlocked new opportunities for education, commerce, and civic engagement. Initiatives such as "Digital India" aim to bridge the digital divide and ensure that technology benefits all citizens. However, rapid technological change also brings challenges. Cybersecurity, data privacy, and equitable access to digital resources are pressing concerns that must be addressed as the nation continues its digital transformation.

Ensuring that the digital revolution contributes to inclusive growth will require robust regulatory frameworks, investment in digital literacy, and initiatives to extend connectivity to remote and underserved areas. As India harnesses the potential of technology, it will also need to manage its risks—an endeavor that calls for both innovation and vigilance.

Global Engagement and the Role of India on the World Stage

Expanding Diplomatic and Economic Horizons

India's emergence as a major global player is reshaping the international order. With its dynamic economy, strategic geopolitical position, and rich cultural heritage, India is increasingly asserting its influence in global affairs. Initiatives such as the "Act East" policy and active participation in multilateral organizations underscore India's commitment to shaping regional and international discourse.

In *In Spite of the Gods*, Edward Luce argues that India's rise is not only an economic phenomenon but also a reflection of its growing geopolitical clout. As India navigates complex relationships with traditional powers and emerging economies alike, it will need to balance national interests with global responsibilities. This balancing act will involve not only economic and military strategy but also the soft power derived from its cultural and democratic values.

Soft Power and Cultural Diplomacy

India's rich cultural legacy is one of its most potent tools for global engagement. The universal appeal of Bollywood films, the global spread of yoga, and the international popularity of Indian cuisine have all contributed to a positive and influential national image. Cultural diplomacy, therefore, plays a crucial role in complementing India's economic and strategic initiatives on the world stage.

As John Keay's *India: A History* demonstrates, India's historical narrative is steeped in cultural exchange and pluralism—qualities that continue to resonate in a globalized world. By leveraging its cultural assets, India can foster deeper ties with other nations, promote mutual understanding, and build a network of partnerships based on shared values. This soft power, when combined with pragmatic economic and political strategies, has the potential to enhance India's standing as a leader in international affairs.

Social Renewal and the Role of Youth

Empowering the Next Generation

One of India's most valuable assets is its young population—a vibrant, dynamic force that is poised to shape the future of the nation. With over half of its citizens under the age of 25, India's youth represent the promise of innovation, creativity, and renewed social energy. However, to fully harness this potential, it is essential to invest in education, skills development, and opportunities for meaningful participation in public life.

The democratization of information and the rise of digital media have given young Indians unprecedented access to global ideas and perspectives. This generation is more connected, more informed, and more eager than ever to drive social change. Policies that promote quality education, vocational training, and entrepreneurship will be key to empowering the next generation. The future of India depends on its ability to provide its youth with the tools they need to thrive in a rapidly changing world.

Social Movements and Grassroots Innovation

Across the country, social movements led by young activists are addressing a range of issues—from environmental protection and gender equality to corruption and social justice. These grassroots initiatives, often fueled by the power of social media, reflect a renewed commitment to democratic participation and civic engagement. They offer hope that the challenges of modern India can be met with fresh ideas and innovative solutions that emerge from the people themselves.

Amartya Sen's *The Argumentative Indian* reminds us that the strength of Indian democracy lies in its capacity for debate and dissent. The active involvement of youth in social and political life not only rejuvenates the democratic process but also ensures that the voices of future generations are heard in the shaping of national policies.

Charting the Road Ahead

A Vision for a Just and Prosperous Society

Looking forward, the path to a brighter future for India is paved with both challenges and opportunities. The nation must continue to build on the foundations of its democratic, pluralistic, and inclusive ethos while addressing pressing issues such as inequality, environmental degradation, and social fragmentation. Achieving a balance between rapid modernization and the preservation of cultural heritage will require visionary leadership, innovative policymaking, and the collective effort of all segments of society.

In envisioning its future, India must strive to create a society where economic prosperity is matched by social justice, where technological advancements contribute to human development, and where global aspirations are tempered by a commitment to sustainable progress. As Granville Austin's *The Indian Constitution: Cornerstone of a Nation* illustrates, the legacy of India's constitutional experiment is not static; it is a living, evolving promise that each generation must work to fulfill.

Policy Innovations and Collaborative Governance

The future of India will also be shaped by its ability to innovate in governance. In an era marked by rapid change and global interdependence, traditional models of administration must be reimagined. Collaborative governance—characterized by partnerships between government, civil society, and the private sector—will be crucial in addressing complex challenges. Policy innovations that promote transparency, accountability, and citizen participation can help ensure that the benefits of progress are shared equitably across society.

Initiatives to promote digital governance, sustainable development, and inclusive education are already underway. By building on these foundations and continuously adapting to new challenges, India can create a governance model that is both responsive and resilient. This approach will be essential for navigating the uncertainties of the future and for realizing the vision of a just and prosperous society.

Concluding Reflections

The journey ahead for India is one of promise, complexity, and profound transformation. Its rich historical legacy—marked by resilience, pluralism, and a capacity for reinvention—provides both a roadmap and an inspiration for the future. As the nation continues to grapple with the challenges of economic inequality, environmental sustainability, and social fragmentation, the enduring ideals of unity, diversity, and democratic participation will remain its guiding lights.

In charting the road ahead, India must draw upon the lessons of its past and the insights of visionary thinkers. The works of Ramachandra Guha, Amartya Sen, John Keay, and Granville Austin, among others, offer invaluable perspectives on how a nation can evolve while staying true to its core values. Their analyses remind us that progress is not a linear process but a dynamic interplay of innovation, adaptation, and collective effort.

As India moves forward into the 21st century, its future will be defined by its ability to harness the potential of its youth, leverage technological advancements for inclusive growth, and engage with the world as a confident, pluralistic democracy. The challenges are formidable, but the spirit of India—a spirit that has weathered millennia of change—remains undiminished. In the words of Jawaharlal Nehru in *The Discovery of India*, "The future beckons to us. Whither do we go and what shall be our endeavor?" It is this enduring question that will continue to drive India's journey into the future—a journey marked by hope, resilience, and the promise of a nation united in diversity.

For those seeking a deeper understanding of this evolving narrative, key texts such as *India After Gandhi* by Ramachandra Guha, *Development as Freedom* by Amartya Sen, *The Indian Constitution: Cornerstone of a Nation* by Granville Austin, and *India: A History* by John Keay provide rich and varied insights into the forces that have shaped modern India and those that will drive its future. These works not only chronicle the remarkable achievements of the past but also offer visions for a future where every citizen can share in the nation's progress.

In conclusion, the road ahead for India is as challenging as it is full of promise. It is a future that demands the courage to innovate, the wisdom to preserve what is valuable, and the collective will to build a society that is just, inclusive, and sustainable. As India writes the next chapter of its long and storied journey, it does so with a deep awareness of its past, an unwavering commitment to its ideals, and a bold vision for the future—a future where unity in diversity is not just a celebrated ideal, but the very foundation upon which a prosperous and harmonious society is built.

www.ingramcontent.com/pod-product-compliance
Lightning Source LLC
Chambersburg PA
CBHW070042230426
43661CB00005B/726